Fools, Liars, Cheaters, *and* Other Bible Heroes

Barbara Hosbach

Franciscan
MEDIA
Cincinnati, Ohio

Cover and book design by Mark Sullivan
Cover image © photoXpress | beawolf

LIBRARY OF CONGRESS CATALOGING-IN-PUBLICATION DATA
Hosbach, Barbara.
Fools, liars, cheaters, and other Bible heroes / Barbara Hosbach.
p. cm.
ISBN 978-1-61636-429-8 (alk. paper)
1. Bible—Biography. I. Title.
BS571.H67 2012
220.9'2—dc23
2012013043

Published by Franciscan Media
28 W. Liberty St.
Cincinnati, OH 45202
www.FranciscanMedia.org

Printed in the United States of America.

Printed on acid-free paper.

12 13 14 15 16   5 4 3 2 1

[• DEDICATION •]

This book is dedicated to the Lord, the Vine
apart from whom we can do nothing.

~ and ~

In memory of my father,
John Bonk,
who taught me to value individuality,
and to my mother,
Mae Pavlosky Bonk,
who shared her love of words with me.

[• ACKNOWLEDGMENTS •]

I want to thank my husband, Raymond Hosbach, for all his loving support as well as for his editorial help. I also want to thank my sister Marie Ruszkay and my friend and colleague Karen Riley, whose encouragement and feedback were invaluable during the writing process. I also thank my sister Carole Hawkins and my friend Christina Huhmann for their ongoing support. Thanks, too, to my daughter, Jennifer Stern, and to my grandson, Joseph Koslowski, who teach me so much about life. I'm also grateful to the Jackson Writers Group, especially Karen Kelly Boyce, for helping me develop as a writer. Finally, I thank everyone with whom I've had the pleasure of working at Franciscan Media. I am very grateful for their interest in this project and for their supportive and expert guidance throughout the publishing process.

[• CONTENTS •]

At first glance it may seem odd to find "fools, liars, and cheaters" as biblical heroes and heroines. The real heroes are the saints and martyrs who fought the good fight, strove for perfection, and, very often, came close to such an ideal—right?

Yet while the saints, these holy men and women, are authentic heroes, we can't overlook those who fought the good fight, failed, failed yet again, but always humbly returned to our Lord seeking forgiveness and mercy. I guess you can say that these are the *imperfect* heroes in our Christian history. You see, the story of the Bible is our story, the human story of flawed people grappling with God, responding to his love, and searching for him in the providence of our daily lives.

In her book, *Fools, Liars, Cheaters, and Other Bible Heroes,* Barbara Hosbach has done a beautiful job of focusing our attention on a few of these characters, and accentuating how God was able to work with them and through them, despite their imperfections and human weaknesses. As St. Paul said in his Second Letter to the Corinthians when asking for relief from a situation which had control over him, "My grace is sufficient for you, for power is made perfect in weakness" (12:9). God's grace was sufficient for them, and it is sufficient for us as well.

God has given us many holy men and women to emulate so that we can reach heavenly glory. But how often, as we read about these amazing people (namely, his most perfect son, Jesus Christ), do we

feel less than perfect? How often do we begin to adopt a defeatist attitude? "That might be fine for St. Thérèse, St. Francis, or Blessed Teresa of Calcutta, but I'm a lowly sinner. How will my life ever mirror theirs?" Sound familiar? This is precisely why God used and continues to use imperfect people to reach out in love to a fallen world, one person at a time.

Fools, Liars, Cheaters, and Other Bible Heroes will acquaint you with both well-known and little-known biblical characters whom God was able to use throughout salvation history, each with their own imperfections. Through their shortcomings, these characters come to life in a way that makes them accessible to scholar and layperson alike. The reflections at the end of each chapter allow the reader to fully enter into the lives of these characters and contemplate how God might be speaking through his word today.

A few of the prickly situations you will find in the book include Rebecca's deception, Miriam's pride, Samuel's difficulty in perceiving God's will, Naaman's arrogance, the demoniac's destructive behavior, and the Samaritan woman's shame. Throughout each account, Hosbach reminds us that God is not limited by our failings.

In addition to these characters with obvious faults, Hosbach brings to light a few characters that are often hidden in the Scriptures to reveal how God was able to use them as well. Ruth's loyalty, Lydia's hospitality, Tabitha's service, and Priscilla, who with her husband became the first couple for Christ, round out some of the heroic tales shared in the book. It is an easy read with insight and commentary that will both enlighten and inspire.

The essential mission of the Church is to evangelize—to bring the Good News of Jesus Christ to every person and in every situation. In today's day and age it can be difficult to do this in our hurting world because of a false notion that God only uses perfect people to accomplish his will.

In *Fools, Liars, Cheaters, and Other Bible Heroes* we can see that God often uses the least likely among us to spread his love and truth. This is a great source of inspiration for those of us who readily recognize our failings and sinfulness. For if God can use these imperfect biblical figures to reveal himself and bring forth goodness and love, than he can certainly use you and me for great things—imperfections and all.

—Allan F. Wright, author of *The Bible's Best Love Stories*

Fools. Liars. Cheaters. Who would expect the likes of these to be invited to the heavenly banquet? But in his parable comparing the kingdom of God to a wedding feast, Jesus tells us that the king invited "both good and bad" (Matthew 22:10). He not only invited people with social standing, but the poor, the disabled, and anybody else his servants could find (see Luke 14:21, 23). Quite an assortment of guests!

The chapters that follow explore the diverse stories of twenty-eight individuals mentioned in Scripture—men and women from both the Old and the New Testaments. Pious or arrogant, famous or unknown, military leader or quiet contemplative—all responded to God's invitation. From Esther, who became queen and saved her people after "enduring" months at a beauty spa, to the outcast madman whose identity was so wrapped up with the demons who plagued him that he called himself "Legion." From Philip, the deacon whose ability to "go with the flow" led him to be in the right place at the right time, to Martha, a type A personality who busily carried out her own agenda. Different personalities. Different circumstances. Different strengths and weaknesses. Yet all were welcomed and called by God to do good works.

"No two snowflakes are alike, and no two people are alike," my dad used to say. God loved each one of us into being, unduplicated from the start. Who better understands how our individual assets and, yes,

even our liabilities can further his kingdom? God knows all about our weaknesses. He calls us anyway.

I hope the stories that follow, along with the questions at the end of each chapter, will encourage us all to embrace our uniqueness and respond more fully to the invitation hidden in the present moment. May we be reassured that God is working in whatever circumstances we find ourselves here and now. Let us reach out to our scriptural mentors for inspiration as the Spirit moves us to join in God's banquet of love.

PART ONE

Old Testament

CHAPTER ONE

Rebecca
Beautiful Bride to Manipulative Mother

Isaac was forty years old when he married Rebekah [Rebecca], daughter of Bethuel the Aramean of Paddan-aram, sister of Laban the Aramean. Isaac prayed to the LORD for his wife, because she was barren; and the LORD granted his prayer, and his wife Rebekah conceived. The children struggled together within her; and she said, "If it is to be this way, why do I live?" So she went to inquire of the LORD. And the LORD said to her,

"Two nations are in your womb,
> and two peoples born of you shall be divided;
the one shall be stronger than the other,
> the elder shall serve the younger."

When her time to give birth was at hand, there were twins in her womb. The first came out red, all his body like a hairy mantle; so they named him Esau. Afterward his brother came out, with his hand gripping Esau's heel; so he was named Jacob. Isaac was sixty years old when she bore them. (Genesis 25:20–26)

Beautiful Bride

Isaac was the son promised to Abraham, the heir through whom God promised to keep his covenant. Living as a foreigner in the promised land of Canaan, Abraham took care to make sure Isaac's wife would be from his own people, so he sent a servant to go back to his homeland to find a bride for Isaac. The servant arrived at the city well where the young women came to get water. There he began to pray and ask God for a specific sign, and his request was answered.

Rebecca, who was young and very beautiful, arrived before he had finished praying. She not only gave him the drink he asked for but watered his camels as well. Here was a young beauty not only willing to serve another when asked but who went the extra mile. When asked, Rebecca didn't hesitate to agree to marry her kinsman, a man she had never laid eyes on. Although arranged marriages were common in that culture, Rebecca's readiness to embrace the unknown is quite notable. She was willing to relocate, to leave her familiar surroundings and live in a land she had never seen. Her family tried to delay her departure, but Abraham's servant was anxious to leave the next day. Rebecca agreed to leave immediately (see Genesis 24:2–58).

Anyone who has relocated because of a spouse's job prospects will appreciate what is involved in taking on such an upheaval with no preparation. This lovely young woman was willing to accommodate the needs of others. When she arrived in Canaan and married Isaac, he was forty years old. Almost twenty years later, Rebecca was still childless. Only after Isaac prayed to the Lord for her did she become pregnant.

Isaac's descendants were to be heirs to God's promise, destined to become the chosen race, the nation set apart by God. St. Paul's Letter to the Romans points out that the choice of one son was completely the result of God's purpose. God told Rebecca that the firstborn son would serve the younger one before the children were even born (see Romans 9:10–12). As we read in the opening Scripture passage, Rebecca felt a struggle within her during her pregnancy.

After twins were born, Isaac preferred Esau, the older son, who grew to be a virile hunter, a "man's man." Rebecca preferred Jacob. My own maternal instinct identifies with the protective urge that may have caused Rebecca to compensate for Isaac's favoritism of Esau. Not only was Esau his father's favorite, but Jacob was probably no physical match for his rugged brother. My heart can understand

wanting to protect a child from being slighted.

Rebecca did what she could to ensure Jacob's well being, but she was living in a man's world. Men owned the property and made the decisions, so she maneuvered behind the scenes. It is not a pretty sight, but she isn't the first or the last mother who manipulated to help her child get ahead.

Perhaps Jacob owed his knack for conniving to his mother's influence. Scripture describes how Jacob got Esau to relinquish all his rights and privileges as firstborn son for a pot of soup. Jacob tantalized his brother with creature comforts. Shady? Maybe so, but Esau also had some responsibility in the matter. Esau chose immediate gratification without considering the long-term effects of his choice (see Genesis 25:29–34).

Manipulative Mother
Rebecca's scheme to get Jacob the special blessing intended for firstborn Esau amounted to outright deception. Isaac had a soft spot in his heart for a favorite stew. He sent Esau out hunting for the game needed to make the special dish. Meanwhile, in Esau's absence, Rebecca cooked up a stew for Jacob to bring to Isaac. She had Jacob disguise himself as Esau by wearing Esau's clothes and simulating his brother's hairy arms with animal skins. Isaac's eyesight was failing so he couldn't tell that Jacob was not Esau. Thus Jacob, having already cheated his brother out of his rights as firstborn son, also stole his blessing (see Genesis 27:1–37).

Rebecca then sought to protect Jacob from his brother's understandable wrath. Ever the manipulator, she used the one sore spot that she and Isaac shared—a dislike of Esau's foreign wives. Rebecca coyly pointed out to Isaac how awful it would be if Jacob also ended up marrying a foreigner. As a result, Isaac sent Jacob to Mesopotamia with his blessing for safety. Out of harm's way, Jacob ended up living with Laban, Rebecca's brother, for many years (Genesis 27:41—28:5).

Although the ends never justify the means, I think Rebecca's heart was in the right place. She wanted to protect the interests of the son she feared was at a disadvantage. But Jacob was the child God had chosen to lead. God had revealed this to Rebecca during her pregnancy (see Genesis 25:23).

I can't help but wonder if Jacob became successful in spite of Rebecca's schemes, rather than because of them. Maybe if she had trusted God more, maybe if she hadn't meddled, Jacob would have succeeded without alienating his brother or being forced to live in exile. Maybe God had to get Jacob out from under his overprotective mother's watchful eye so he could develop as a leader in his own right. Jacob had his own struggles and triumphs while living with his uncle, ultimately fathering twelve sons who became the heads of the twelve tribes of Israel, the Chosen People (see Genesis 35:22–26; Exodus 1:1–7).

Only Human

I can relate to the very human emotions that Rebecca might have felt. Nothing else explains to me how the helpful young wife degenerated into a manipulating mother. Rebecca's actions and style were clearly less than perfect. Nevertheless, God worked through her to fulfill his plan.

Even today, although parents may love their children equally, natural preferences still enter into the human heart. Feelings are not sins, but that doesn't relieve us of the responsibility to act fairly. When favoritism dominates family relationships, polarizations and divisions can occur.

Well-meant, but misguided or overdeveloped protective instincts can also do more harm than good. As our children grow, we can feel threatened as they begin finding their own way without us. This sometimes includes allowing them to experience the consequences of their choices. Praying for wisdom, seeking guidance from trusted

role models or professionals, and remembering that God loves our children even more than we do can all support our parenting efforts.

Parents aren't the only ones tempted to take matters into their own hands. When God's will doesn't match our plans it is easy to forget that he has everything under control. Scripture is filled with God's reassurance. One example is when God told the prophet Jeremiah that he alone knew his plans for his people, plans for prosperity rather than calamity, plans for a hope-filled future (see Jeremiah 29:11).

The psalmist tells us that if we look to God for our happiness, he will give us our heart's desire (see Psalm 37:4). In spite of this promise, when our yearning for a healthy relationship seems to go unanswered, loneliness can get the best of us. At those times, we may make choices that are not in the best interests of others or ourselves.

When people—at work, at home, on the road—don't act the way we think they should, our goal can easily become getting them to see or do things our way. Even when we are only trying to help, such maneuvers usually create tension and become self-defeating. No matter how loving our motives may be, it never helps when we try to force outcomes. At those times, we may well be part of the problem rather than the solution.

Ultimately, none of us is powerful enough to thwart God's plans. He knows all about our lack of trust. He knows we mean well. I believe he takes that into account and uses us to accomplish his will anyway, just as he did with Rebecca.

Questions for Reflection and Discussion

1. God told Rebecca about his plans for Jacob and Esau before they were born. When have his plans and provisions for you unfolded before you became aware of it?

2. How do you think feelings may have motivated Rebecca's actions on Jacob's behalf?

3. Think of a time when you attempted to control the outcome of a situation. What feelings were involved? How did it turn out?

4. Why is it important to remember that God has everything under control? Name some resources that can remind you of this.

5. How do you know when to act and when to "let go and let God?"

CHAPTER TWO

Leah

Second-Best in Her Husband's Eyes

Now Laban had two daughters; the name of the elder was Leah, and the name of the younger was Rachel. Leah's eyes were lovely, and Rachel was graceful and beautiful. Jacob loved Rachel; so he said, "I will serve you seven years for your younger daughter Rachel." Laban said, "It is better that I give her to you than that I should give her to any other man; stay with me." So Jacob served seven years for Rachel, and they seemed to him but a few days because of the love he had for her.

Then Jacob said to Laban, "Give me my wife that I may go in to her, for my time is completed." So Laban gathered together all the people of the place, and made a feast. But in the evening he took his daughter Leah and brought her to Jacob; and he went in to her. (Laban gave his maid Zilpah to his daughter Leah to be her maid.) When morning came, it was Leah! And Jacob said to Laban, "What is this you have done to me? Did I not serve with you for Rachel? Why then have you deceived me?" Laban said, "This is not done in our country—giving the younger before the firstborn. Complete the week of this one, and we will give you the other also in return for serving me another seven years." Jacob did so, and completed her week; then Laban gave him his daughter Rachel as a wife. (Laban gave his maid Bilhah to his daughter Rachel to be her maid.) So Jacob went in to Rachel also, and he loved Rachel more than Leah. He served Laban for another seven years.

When the LORD saw that Leah was unloved, he opened
her womb; but Rachel was barren. (Genesis 29:16–31)

No Competition

In spite of her lovely eyes, Leah was clearly no competition for her
younger and more attractive sister Rachel. No one offered to work
seven years to win Leah's hand in marriage. That would have been
bad enough. Then her father palmed her off as the daughter Jacob
had worked for. How humiliating! Jacob's anger at being cheated
is understandable, but how did it feel to be on the receiving end of
Jacob's disappointment and resentment? How much rejection can a
woman take?

Although having more than one wife was common in that culture,
making room for Rachel, clearly the favorite, had to be bitterly painful
for Leah. But God, in his goodness and wisdom, blessed Leah. She
may have not been graced with physical beauty, but she was able to
bear six sons: Reuben, Simeon, Levi, Judah, Issachar, and Zebulun, as
well as a daughter, Dinah.

Leah's fruitfulness secured her a position of respect. Rachel, childless, thus had reason to be jealous of her sister until Rachel, much
later, finally became pregnant. Rachel gave birth to Joseph, and finally
to Benjamin, who became Jacob's favorite sons (see Genesis 30:22–
24; 35:16–18).

Leah, although respected, probably never felt cherished as Rachel
did. I suspect that circumstances forced Leah to grow in the kind of
humility that builds character. This opportunity for character development may have been part of God's plan. I wonder how much influence Leah had on her sons?

It seems likely her firstborn, Reuben, empathized with the plight of
her second-rate status. When he found mandrakes, a plant thought
to be a love or fertility charm, he brought them to his mother (see
Genesis 30:14) Could it be that witnessing his mother's status also
developed Reuben's sensitivity to the sorrow of others? Later, he was

instrumental at saving Rachel's son Joseph from the wrath of his brothers (see Genesis 37:21–22).

Leah's plight and her response to it might have provided an important example to her children. After all, it was not through Jacob's favorite wife or favorite sons that the promised Messiah came: It was through Leah's son, Judah. The book of Revelation refers to Jesus as "the Lion of the tribe of Judah" (5:5). God also chose the tribe of Leah's son Levi in lieu of the firstborn sons of Israel. Members of the tribe of Levi were appointed by God to serve in the tent of God's presence (see Numbers 3:5–13).

God's ways are not our ways, and his choices are not ours. God allowed Leah to become Jacob's wife for a reason, in spite of Jacob's preference. She may have lacked the luster of physical beauty, but I believe Leah had the luster of character. If Leah had not faced emotional challenges, I wonder how that might have influenced her development?

Perhaps she would not have had the strength of character needed to be the mother of tribes destined to play such a huge role in God's plan. Still, at the time, that might have felt like small compensation for not feeling cherished by her husband.

Working Through Rejection

We've all felt the pain of rejection. Some of those hurts may have come early in life—a parent's preferential treatment of a brother or sister, or not making the team or the "in crowd" at school. Other rejections may come later in life. The person we wanted to marry had other ideas. We may have been passed over for an important job or promotion.

Maybe a spouse abandoned us (if not physically, perhaps emotionally). Harsh or perpetual criticism can be devastating. We all crave emotional satisfaction. It isn't easy to endure rejection in any form. Hurt and disappointment are normal and understandable reactions.

We don't have to pretend we don't feel them. But we aren't doomed to misery.

While it is appropriate to sort out and take responsibility for our part in situations, it isn't always about us exclusively. It is helpful to balance self-examination with focusing elsewhere. Just because one person, one employer, or one group isn't interested in what we have to offer at a certain point in time, it doesn't mean we have nothing to offer.

The more we focus on what God's plan for us might be, the less we need to concern ourselves with other people's reactions. Our self-worth is not dependent on other people's opinions of us. No one else has the power to make us better or worse than we are. Only our choices can do that. We are here because the God who gave us free will also loved us into existence. It is not easy to remember this without some outside validation to help us. That might be why God created us to live in community. Just as he did for Leah, he will always provide what we need.

Questions for Reflection and Discussion

1. Imagine yourself in Leah's place. How would you respond to Jacob's response after the deception? How would you feel if you were the one to bear several children, while your sister could not? What challenges do you think these events might have brought with them?

2. What coping skills might have helped Leah deal with these situations? How can these coping skills help when you or those around you experience rejection?

3. Where can you turn for support when you need affirmation? How can you find or develop a support network?

4. How has God brought validation or some other good to you at a time when other people did not or could not validate you?

5. Have there been times when you have rejected others—perhaps without even realizing it? How might you make amends?

CHAPTER THREE

Reuben
A Man of Conscience

And Israel said to Joseph, "Are not your brothers pasturing the flock at Shechem? Come, I will send you to them." He answered, "Here I am."... They saw him from a distance, and before he came near to them, they conspired to kill him. They said to one another, "Here comes this dreamer. Come now, let us kill him and throw him into one of the pits; then we shall say that a wild animal has devoured him, and we shall see what will become of his dreams." But when Reuben heard it, he delivered him out of their hands, saying, "Let us not take his life." Reuben said to them, "Shed no blood; throw him into this pit here in the wilderness, but lay no hand on him"—that he might rescue him out of their hand and restore him to his father. So when Joseph came to his brothers, they stripped him of his robe, the long robe with sleeves that he wore; and they took him and threw him into a pit. The pit was empty; there was no water in it.

Then they sat down to eat; and looking up they saw a caravan of Ishmaelites coming from Gilead, with their camels carrying gum, balm, and resin, on their way to carry it down to Egypt. Then Judah said to his brothers, "What profit is it if we kill our brother and conceal his blood? Come, let us sell him to the Ishmaelites, and not lay our hands on him, for he is our brother, our own flesh." And his brothers agreed. When some Midianite traders passed by, they drew Joseph up, lifting him out of the pit, and sold him to the Ishmaelites for twenty pieces of silver. And they took Joseph to Egypt.

When Reuben returned to the pit and saw that Joseph was not in the pit, he tore his clothes. He returned to his brothers, and said, "The boy is gone; and I, where can I turn?" Then they took Joseph's robe, slaughtered a goat, and dipped the robe in the blood. They had the long robe with sleeves taken to their father, and they said, "This we have found; see now whether it is your son's robe or not." He recognized it, and said, "It is my son's robe! A wild animal has devoured him; Joseph is without doubt torn to pieces." (Genesis 37:13, 18–33)

Following His Conscience

When his father sent Joseph to check up on them, his brothers planned to kill him. Only Reuben, of all the brothers, intervened. This was remarkable. Reuben must have had as much natural dislike for Joseph as his brothers. Moreover, Reuben was the firstborn son. He was the oldest child of Jacob's first wife, Leah, entitled to the privileges of the firstborn. Reuben, more than the others, had reason to feel threatened by Jacob's preference for the young Joseph. Yet he stood up for Joseph against the majority, aligning himself against nine angry men.

Reuben followed his conscience, although he could only do so much. He couldn't stop the head of steam his brothers had worked up, but he did what he could. He bought time. Because he convinced the others to put Joseph in a dry well rather than kill him on the spot, Reuben created the opportunity for hope. He planned to help Joseph get back home safely when he got the chance. Although things did not work out as Reuben envisioned, his action furthered God's plan.

Joseph was eventually sold into slavery and ended up in Egypt. His gift for dream interpretation ultimately brought him to the attention of the pharaoh. He correctly interpreted the pharaoh's dream as a warning against coming famine and gained the highest-ranking position as Pharaoh's right-hand man.

Joseph's administrative skills allowed him to organize the stockpiling and rationing of grain. He thereby saved the population of Egypt and countless others—including his family back in Canaan—from starvation. Such was the vision, extraordinary talent, and remarkable events that were part of God's plan for Joseph (see Genesis 39–47).

None of it would have happened if Reuben had not acted on his conscience. He overcame his natural resentment of Joseph and the precariousness of his own position as firstborn. He mustered the courage to stand against his brothers' united front. Reuben didn't do it because he knew Joseph was going to do great things and be the savior of his family and entire nations. Nor did he do it to get his name recorded in history. Reuben did it because he couldn't live with himself or with his father's grief if anything happened to Joseph. Things didn't work out as Reuben hoped, but his inspiring action and courage furthered God's awesome saving plan.

Making the Right Choice
We never know what repercussions our actions will have. It takes tremendous courage to follow what we know to be right, to oppose popular opinion, or even to oppose our own families. For example, breaking the code of silence in a family denying or hiding the pain of alcoholism, addiction, or incest can be terrifying. When a family member seeking help dares to share the torment of reality in a responsible way—such as with a therapist or at a Twelve Step meeting—other family members may turn on that person. Seeking help is not being disloyal. It is an act of bravery.

Our actions may never make headlines. Not all of us are called or have the opportunity to be heroes in a dramatic way. But every time we make the hard right choice or extend ourselves in some life-giving way, we are helping to save the world. Like Reuben, we can take the right action without knowing or even thinking about what the ramifications will be for that person or ourselves down the road.

Stories abound of people going down for the last time—sometimes physically, sometimes emotionally or spiritually—that were buoyed up by another to just take one more step. And that step led to another, and another, as the person grew past their desperation and became a contributor to the positive force of life.

You may recall times that you or someone you know showed courage in the face of opposition. On the other hand, maybe like me, you regret missed opportunities to stand up for what was right. Both memories can motivate us as we continue to grow. After all, Reuben took action to save Joseph, but still participated in the cover-up. He stood with his brothers in telling their father that Joseph had been killed by a wild animal. I wonder what influence the memories of Reuben's actions had on his subsequent choices.

Other biblical figures lacked the courage of their convictions at times but later served the Lord with renewed dedication. Perhaps the most famous is Peter, whose denial of Jesus is recorded in all four Gospels (Matthew 26:69–75; Mark 14:66–72; Luke 22:54–62; and John 18:15–18, 25–27). Yet later, Peter boldly led the early Church in the face of challenges and threats (Acts 4:1–30).

Peter wasn't perfect. Reuben wasn't perfect either, but he did the best he could—just like us.

Questions for Reflection and Discussion

1. Before taking a stand for what you believe is right, what are some important things to consider?
2. How can you learn to see God working when you have taken a risk in good conscience and things don't turn out as you had hoped?
3. Why is it important to forgive yourself for the times you have failed to stand up for what was right?
4. What can help you forgive yourself and others for falling short of your expectations?

CHAPTER FOUR

Miriam
Prophetess With an Opportunity

While they were at Hazeroth, Miriam and Aaron spoke against Moses because of the Cushite woman whom he had married (for he had indeed married a Cushite woman); and they said, "Has the LORD spoken only through Moses? Has he not spoken through us also?" And the LORD heard it. Now the man Moses was very humble, more so than anyone else on the face of the earth. Suddenly the LORD said to Moses, Aaron, and Miriam, "Come out, you three, to the tent of meeting." So the three of them came out. Then the LORD came down in a pillar of cloud, and stood at the entrance of the tent, and called Aaron and Miriam; and they both came forward. And he said, "Hear my words:

When there are prophets among you,
   I the LORD make myself known to them in visions;
   I speak to them in dreams.
Not so with my servant Moses;
   he is entrusted with all my house.
With him I speak face to face—clearly, not in riddles;
   and he beholds the form of the LORD.
Why then were you not afraid to speak against my servant Moses?" And the anger of the LORD was kindled against them, and he departed.

When the cloud went away from over the tent, Miriam had become leprous, as white as snow. And Aaron turned towards Miriam and saw that she was leprous. Then Aaron said to Moses, "Oh, my lord, do not punish us for a sin that

we have so foolishly committed. Do not let her be like one stillborn, whose flesh is half consumed when it comes out of its mother's womb." And Moses cried to the LORD, "O God, please heal her." But the LORD said to Moses, "If her father had but spit in her face, would she not bear her shame for seven days? Let her be shut out of the camp for seven days, and after that she may be brought in again."

So Miriam was shut out of the camp for seven days; and the people did not set out on the march until Miriam had been brought in again. (Numbers 12:1–15)

Ms. Understood

Miriam was not a bad person. She watched over her baby brother Moses when their mother placed him in a basket in the Nile River to save him from death under the Egyptian decree. When Pharaoh's daughter found him, it was Miriam who suggested a Hebrew wet nurse. She thereby arranged for Moses to be nursed by his own mother, while being brought up under the protection of Pharaoh's court (see Exodus 2:4–8).

Miriam is referred to as a prophetess. After Moses led the Hebrews through the Red Sea and God destroyed their Egyptian enemies, Miriam led the other women in a musical celebration, singing God's praise for the victory. She was obviously aware of and grateful for God's power working to save the Hebrew nation (see Exodus 15:20–21).

If it weren't for Miriam's protection when Moses was an infant, there might not even have been an Exodus. Was she really out of line in considering herself equal to Moses? It is understandable that Miriam felt justified in looking down on her little brother, especially since he had married an outsider.

So why was Miriam, and not Aaron (who also criticized Moses) afflicted with a horrifying skin disease and exiled for seven days?

Perhaps God knew Miriam's heart needed a more direct experience in order to be softened.

The above passage from Numbers makes a point of saying that Moses was humble, more humble than anyone else on earth. Maybe that is the key. Miriam had an active role in God's salvation plan and she definitely played her part. But that part was clearly less prominent than Moses's role.

Could competition be the crux of the issue? Miriam served God in the way she was called. Moses had a riskier, weightier role to play, but he was humble about it. His position of leadership made him more aware of his human limitations. He keenly felt his need for God and for another, his brother, Aaron, to assist him. Moses didn't need to build himself up by comparing his worth to that of others.

Apparently, Miriam did. She looked down on Moses for marrying an outsider. She joined Aaron in claiming equal footing with Moses as God's spokesperson. Self-righteousness and the insecurity that breeds it are very common. People who feel good about themselves don't need to build their self-esteem at the expense of others. Miriam felt the need to emphasize her own importance. She could not see that who she was was enough; that being faithful to the promptings she received was sufficient, that her role was important enough without comparisons or recognition.

Humility Versus Self-Esteem

If ever a person had reason to get a big head, it was Moses, but he had humility. It is good to acknowledge our talents and abilities. Healthy self-esteem is built on this. Humility does not mean thinking bad things about ourselves or dwelling on our inadequacies.

Paradoxically, being aware of our limitations can build self-esteem as we recognize that our abilities and talents are God given. We are then free to use them, not for our own aggrandizement, but to serve. Humility can also guide us in setting realistic goals for ourselves and

prevent the discouragement that comes when we fail to live up to our own grandiose expectations.

Miriam's disease and her seven days of solitude outside the camp gave her an opportunity for reflection. We aren't told how she might have changed after returning to the camp. No doubt the experience forced her to face her limitations, her true relationship with God, and the fact that the little brother she had looked down on was the one whose prayers helped restore her to health.

Although humbled, perhaps Miriam developed the true healthy self-esteem that comes from recognizing that self-worth does not depend on prominence or impressive achievements. Despite her foibles and affliction, the entire Hebrew nation waited for Miriam before they moved on. She was not abandoned. She had inherent value as a person, by God's grace. This is good news for those of us that feel driven to build our weak self-images up by externals or by belittling others, even in our own minds.

Maybe that's why Jesus warned us that those who tried to gain honor for themselves would be humbled and those who humbled themselves would be made great (Luke 14:11). We don't have to struggle to make ourselves great. It doesn't work. But we will be built up as we recognize that we have value in spite of our weaknesses. We are worthy of love simply because we are God's creation.

Questions for Reflection and Discussion

1. Miriam led others in praising God for victory over Israel's enemies, but criticized her brother Moses. What problems can arise when you praise God while judging others?

2. What is humility? How does it differ from humiliation or from putting yourself down? How can you grow in humility?

3. When Miriam was shut out of the camp for seven days, the others waited for her before moving on. Have there been times when

others were held back from moving on because of your actions? Have there been times when you have been held back from moving on because of someone else?

4. Are you being called at the present time to wait patiently for someone or some situation to resolve before moving on? How do you know when it is time to move on?

CHAPTER FIVE

Rahab
Liar, Gentile, and Prostitute

Then Joshua son of Nun sent two men secretly from Shittim as spies, saying, "Go, view the land, especially Jericho." So they went, and entered the house of a prostitute whose name was Rahab, and spent the night there. The king of Jericho was told, "Some Israelites have come here tonight to search out the land." Then the king of Jericho sent orders to Rahab, "Bring out the men who have come to you, who entered your house, for they have come only to search out the whole land." But the woman took the two men and hid them. Then she said, "True, the men came to me, but I did not know where they came from. And when it was time to close the gate at dark, the men went out. Where the men went I do not know. Pursue them quickly, for you can overtake them." She had, however, brought them up to the roof and hidden them with the stalks of flax that she had laid out on the roof. So the men pursued them on the way to the Jordan as far as the fords. As soon as the pursuers had gone out, the gate was shut.

Before they went to sleep, she came up to them on the roof and said to the men: "I know that the LORD has given you the land, and that dread of you has fallen on us, and that all the inhabitants of the land melt in fear before you. For we have heard how the LORD dried up the water of the Red Sea before you when you came out of Egypt, and what you did to the two kings of the Amorites that were beyond the Jordan, to Sihon and Og, whom you utterly destroyed. As soon as we heard it, our hearts melted, and there was no courage left in

any of us because of you. The LORD your God is indeed God in heaven above and on earth below. Now then, since I have dealt kindly with you, swear to me by the LORD that you in turn will deal kindly with my family. Give me a sign of good faith that you will spare my father and mother, my brothers and sisters, and all who belong to them, and deliver our lives from death."…

The men said to her, "We will be released from this oath that you have made us swear to you if we invade the land and you do not tie this crimson cord in the window through which you let us down, and you do not gather into your house your father and mother, your brothers, and all your family. If any of you go out of the doors of your house into the street, they shall be responsible for their own death, and we shall be innocent; but if a hand is laid upon any who are with you in the house, we shall bear the responsibility for their death. But if you tell this business of ours, then we shall be released from this oath that you made us swear to you." She said, "According to your words, so be it." She sent them away and they departed. Then she tied the crimson cord in the window. (Joshua 2:1–13, 17–21)

Rahab, Lying, Gentile Prostitute

A lying, Gentile prostitute! And yet Rahab and her family were the only ones spared in the whole town of Jericho (see Joshua 6:24–25). Joshua and his army kept the promise that had been made to Rahab. They owed her. Thanks to her assistance, the two Israelite spies were able to return to their camp with valuable information that Rahab had provided about her countrymen's state of mind.

It is easy to think Rahab's actions were self-serving and that she just wanted to be on the side of the winners. Women who sell themselves for money probably get used to looking out for number one. But a closer look tells us more.

The risk Rahab took was real. Lying to the authorities was not playing it safe. She risked her own skin. Had her deception been discovered—as it well might have been—the king's fury would have been savage. Rahab also risked trusting strangers—enemy spies—to keep their word. In her line of work, Rahab probably met men who lied all the time. These enemy spies could have escaped and, in spite of her help, forgotten all about her.

What made Rahab take her chances with the spies? It was her faith in the God of the Israelites. She told the spies that she, along with everyone else in the country, had heard how God had protected the Israelites and given them victory after leading them out of Egyptian bondage. Convinced of his power, Rahab affirms that the God of Israel is the Lord of heaven and earth.

It is ironic that the Israelite community, who experienced God's saving power firsthand, continued to complain and doubt in the desert, while this foreign woman from the wrong side of the tracks was convinced enough to convert based only on hearing the testimony of others. Rahab heard about God's power and was willing to give up her home, along with all that was familiar to her. She placed her future in the hands of the God she had only heard about and the people he chose to work through. She bet her life, and the lives of her loved ones, on God.

The author of the letter to the Hebrews must have seen the same thing, for he said that it was Rahab's faith that protected her from death because she welcomed the Israelite spies (see Hebrews 11:31). By sheltering them, she put her faith into action. When James wrote that it is not only faith, but also our actions that are involved in having

a right relationship with God, he used Rahab as an example of faith being shown through action (James 2:24–25).

Living Our Faith

We are not saved by our standing in the community, or by our lack of it. We are saved by our faith—faith that springs from honest awareness of our need for God. But that is not enough. We must then trust him enough to follow his instructions. If we don't follow his directions, we may walk out of his protection.

Rahab and her family were saved because she trusted enough to follow instructions. Rahab put the red cord in her window as a sign, although there was a chance it might have aroused questions or suspicions among her neighbors. She convinced her family to stay within her house, as she had been warned. This made it possible for her protectors to guarantee her safety.

Unlike Lot's wife, or the Israelites when they left Egypt, Rahab did not keep looking back with longing to the ruins of her old life. We are told that she became so acculturated within the Israelite community that her descendants were still living there when the book of Joshua was finally recorded in writing (Joshua 6:25). Presumably this was long after the events occurred. The genealogy listed in Matthew names Rahab as one of the ancestors of David, and ultimately of Jesus (Matthew 1:5). God truly does move in mysterious ways and he works through whomever he chooses.

In one sense, choosing God is always self-serving. Since he has our greatest good in mind, how could it be anything else? If I wait to choose God out of purely noble motives, solely because it is the right thing to do, I am going to be waiting a long time. I am dependent on God for the very air I breathe, for life itself. I did not create myself.

But choosing God is still the right choice to make and we all get many opportunities to make that choice every day. Rahab made that choice and never looked back.

Questions for Reflection and Discussion

1. Rahab's sins and low standing in the community did not keep her from serving God and helping others. When has an unlikely person or group come to your assistance?

2. Have you ever felt intimidated by the credentials of other people or held back from helping others because you felt you lacked qualifications? What are some ways to deal with this?

3. How can you avoid focusing on your past mistakes and turn your attention to what God is calling you to do in the present?

4. Once you have taken an action you felt was the right thing to do, how can you keep from looking back and second-guessing your choice?

CHAPTER SIX

Deborah
Unlikely Leader on the Battlefield

Then the Israelites cried out to the LORD for help; for [Sisera] had nine hundred chariots of iron, and had oppressed the Israelites cruelly for twenty years.

At that time Deborah, a prophetess, wife of Lappidoth, was judging Israel. She used to sit under the palm of Deborah between Ramah and Bethel in the hill country of Ephraim; and the Israelites came up to her for judgment. She sent and summoned Barak son of Abinoam from Kedesh in Naphtali, and said to him, "The LORD, the God of Israel, commands you, 'Go, take position at Mount Tabor, bringing ten thousand from the tribe of Naphtali and the tribe of Zebulun. I will draw out Sisera, the general of Jabin's army, to meet you by the Wadi Kishon with his chariots and his troops; and I will give him into your hand.'" Barak said to her, "If you will go with me, I will go; but if you will not go with me, I will not go." And she said, "I will surely go with you; nevertheless, the road on which you are going will not lead to your glory, for the LORD will sell Sisera into the hand of a woman." Then Deborah got up and went with Barak to Kedesh.

Barak summoned Zebulun and Naphtali to Kedesh; and ten thousand warriors went up behind him; and Deborah went up with him....

Then Deborah said to Barak, "Up! For this is the day on which the LORD has given Sisera into your hand. The LORD is indeed going out before you." So Barak went down from Mount Tabor with ten thousand warriors following him. And

the LORD threw Sisera and all his chariots and all his army into a panic before Barak; Sisera got down from his chariot and fled away on foot, while Barak pursued the chariots and the army to Harosheth-ha-goiim. All the army of Sisera fell by the sword; no one was left. (Judges 4:3–10, 14–16)

A Woman of Words and Action

There are strong women mentioned in both Old and New Testaments. Many worked behind the scenes, or within the restrictions placed by the men in authority over them. Few are mentioned that held such a position of leadership in a male-dominated culture as Deborah. People valued her wisdom and insight in spite of the fact that she was a woman. Portrayed as a community leader, it seems even more unusual to see Deborah's apparent authority over a military leader. When she sent for Barak, he came. She told him what God had commanded: Barak had been chosen to lead the Israelites to victory against their oppressors.

Barak's refusal to go unless Deborah went with him sounds almost childlike. I doubt that Barak wanted a hand to hold. Despite being a community leader, Deborah, as a woman, would not have been expected to march toward the battlefield. It is easy to say, "God told me that you should do such and such," when the speaker is not the one in harm's way. Who can blame Barak for wanting a show of good faith on Deborah's part?

Not all Israelites were willing to fight against their Canaanite oppressors. Several tribes did not participate in the campaign (see Judges 5:15–17). Barak was willing to venture into battle once Deborah backed up her words with action. She trusted God's message and her willingness to act on that trust empowered Barak to do the same. Barak's courage in turn inspired others to follow.

Although Barak led the Israelite army to victory against the

Canaanites, Sisera, the Canaanite leader, fled on foot and was ultimately killed by another woman, Jael, while sleeping in her tent (see Judges 4:17–22). Deborah had predicted this. Nevertheless, it is Barak, not Deborah, listed in the litany of faithful leaders by the author of Hebrews (Hebrews 11:32).

On the other hand, Deborah is the only woman leader mentioned in the book of Judges. The inclusion of her story in the Bible confirms that God uses whomever he chooses for his purpose. He can work wonders when people have sufficient trust in his plan to go against the considerable tide of the way things have always been.

A Model of Courage

Deborah's wisdom had already been established. People sought her out for advice. I wonder how her husband felt about people seeking out his wife's words of wisdom rather than his. I wonder if some of the prominent men in her community felt threatened and grumbled against her. How much courage did it take for her to accept a role as leader in spite of being a woman?

Deborah's courage was not just shown in her willingness to stick her neck out on a battlefield. It was shown in her willingness to step out and be true to what she felt God was calling her to do, in spite of cultural restrictions. Her courage may have started the first time she said yes to that inner nudge and risked sharing the truth and wisdom she received with just one other person.

Women aren't the only ones who are challenged to step beyond the status quo. It is tempting to tune out inner promptings that invite us to venture where we have never gone before. It is OK to start small. Deborah wasn't born automatically dispensing judgments under that palm tree. Her destiny probably evolved gradually as she chose to say yes to each small challenge along the way.

Not all of us are called to a prominent role in society. Whether our choices impact the world or just our little corner of it, we can still

make a difference. Willingness to act outside the norm—when it is part of God's plan for us—prepares us to act with more courage in the future and may inspire others as well.

Questions for Reflection and Discussion

1. The people of Israel sought out Deborah for her decisions. What qualities does a discerning judge need? What evidence of these qualities do you see in Deborah's interactions with Barak?

2. Along with being a prophet and judge, Deborah was also the wife of Lappidoth. What challenges do you think she might have faced between her role in the community and her home life? What do you think would have helped her meet these challenges? Are there similar challenges in your life?

3. In accompanying Barak to Kedesh, Deborah displayed courage, which inspired Barak to follow her lead. He, in turn, was followed by others. Have you ever taken an action or witnessed someone else take an action that inspired others to follow? What prompted that initial action?

4. For a woman in her culture, Deborah ventured beyond the status quo. Name some people who have challenged the status quo in society. Do you admire any of them? Why?

5. Challenging the status quo doesn't always involve dramatic situations or gain widespread attention. Are you being called to move beyond "the way things have always been" in some area of your life? Is anything holding you back from making that change? What can help you overcome that obstacle?

CHAPTER SEVEN

Gideon
Soldier of God

Then the LORD turned to him and said, "Go in this might of
yours and deliver Israel from the hand of Midian; I hereby
commission you." He responded, "But sir, how can I deliver
Israel? My clan is the weakest in Manasseh, and I am the
least in my family." The LORD said to him, "But I will be with
you, and you shall strike down the Midianites, every one of
them."...

The LORD said to Gideon, "The troops with you are too
many for me to give the Midianites into their hand. Israel
would only take the credit away from me, saying, 'My own
hand has delivered me.' Now therefore proclaim this in the
hearing of the troops, 'Whoever is fearful and trembling, let
him return home.'" Thus Gideon sifted them out; twenty-
two thousand returned, and ten thousand remained.

Then the LORD said to Gideon, "The troops are still too
many; take them down to the water and I will sift them out
for you there. When I say, 'This one shall go with you,' he
shall go with you; and when I say, 'This one shall not go with
you,' he shall not go." So he brought the troops down to the
water; and the LORD said to Gideon, "All those who lap the
water with their tongues, as a dog laps, you shall put to one
side; all those who kneel down to drink, putting their hands
to their mouths, you shall put to the other side." The number
of those that lapped was three hundred; but all the rest of
the troops knelt down to drink water. Then the LORD said to
Gideon, "With the three hundred that lapped I will deliver

you, and give the Midianites into your hand. Let all the others go to their homes." So he took the jars of the troops from their hands, and their trumpets; and he sent all the rest of Israel back to their own tents, but retained the three hundred. The camp of Midian was below him in the valley.

When they blew the three hundred trumpets, the LORD set every man's sword against his fellow and against all the army; and the army fled as far as Beth-shittah toward Zererah, as far as the border of Abel-meholah, by Tabbath. (Judges 6:14–16; 7:2–8, 22)

Strength in God

Gideon wondered how he could possibly rescue Israel. He was a nobody—even his family didn't have any clout. His seeming insignificance didn't worry God, though. For it is God's strength, not ours, that matters. If we supply the willingness, God supplies the power to do whatever he calls us to do.

Gideon became a man on a mission, amassing an army of thirty-two thousand—far too many for God's purposes. To eliminate misplaced faith in numbers, God had Gideon send home those who were afraid. Although those twenty-two thousand had been willing in spite of their fear, it was not God's plan for them to fight—at least not in that battle.

Even though it was a huge loss, eliminating those who were afraid made psychological sense. Cowardice and desertion on the front lines might have been contagious. Nevertheless, Gideon's force had been reduced by two-thirds. Surely now he was stepping out in faith, wasn't he? Nope. Still too many. God instructed Gideon to reduce the army further, selecting those few who were to remain and fight by the way they drank water.

If Gideon tried to follow the logic in that seemingly arbitrary process, he probably didn't get too far. But God led Gideon step by step.

Elsewhere in Judges, we're told that prior to this incident, Gideon asked for and received several signs from God (see Judges 6:17–22, 36–40). So by this point, Gideon may have been more willing to trust God without understanding. Judges 7—8 details the victory of Gideon and the Israelites over the Midianites.

Battle Call

What does Gideon's story have to do with us? Most of us aren't soldiers. Besides, if God is love, why would he train and prepare us for battle? Maybe we need to stand up for ourselves in an abusive relationship or an unacceptable work environment. Maybe we're being called to resist the enemy voices in our own heads—voices that bully us or camouflage themselves as false humility, telling us we dare not venture outside our comfort zone. "I'm not good enough," isn't humility speaking; it's fear.

Taking a risk to try something new can be an act of faith if we believe it's part of God's plan for us. He would not have prompted us if he didn't think we had all we needed for the task at hand—including the necessary skills and whatever external support the situation would require. Confidence isn't pride when we recognize our abilities as God-given and remain grateful to the Giver.

So often, our fear of not being good enough drives us to overcompensate. For example, when we host a holiday meal, we may buy and cook enough food to feed an army. It can happen with intangibles, too. When we rely on our own strength, sooner or later, we're bound to come up against our very real, very human limitations. So we try too hard, keeping a mental resume of accomplishments to prove our worth. We don't have to try so hard.

While we all need encouragement, sometimes we may rely a bit too much on others. Maybe we're afraid to join a gym or a support group if we can't convince someone to go with us. We don't have to be so afraid.

We are enough because God is with us. Just as Gideon's reinforcements were whittled down, maybe our familiar supports fall away for one reason or another. When we're left facing our own weakness, there's nothing else to do but call on God's strength. Whatever fears we've faced in the past, we've survived them all. The support we were looking for at the time may not have been there. That doesn't mean God wasn't supporting us. After all, we did get through. That same God will always provide what we need—both the internal resources and external assistance—to get through anything he has in mind for us.

Questions for Reflection and Discussion

1. When the Lord told Gideon, "You can do it because I will help you," what type of help do you think Gideon expected?

2. God told Gideon that the men he had were too many because they might have thought they had won by themselves and not have given God the credit. Why would thinking they had won by themselves not have been in the men's best interests?

3. Although the Lord reduced Gideon's army, he didn't eliminate it. Gideon didn't fight the enemy alone. What is a healthy balance between seeking and accepting help without being overly dependent on others?

4. Are you being called to do battle against some oppressive force—either internal or external—in your life? If so, how can Gideon's story help you address the issue?

CHAPTER EIGHT

Ruth
Foreign Widow, Loyal Israelite

In the days when the judges ruled, there was a famine in the land, and a certain man of Bethlehem in Judah went to live in the country of Moab, he and his wife and two sons. The name of the man was Elimelech and the name of his wife Naomi, and the names of his two sons were Mahlon and Chilion; they were Ephrathites from Bethlehem in Judah. They went into the country of Moab and remained there. But Elimelech, the husband of Naomi, died, and she was left with her two sons. These took Moabite wives; the name of the one was Orpah and the name of the other Ruth. When they had lived there for about ten years, both Mahlon and Chilion also died, so that the woman was left without her two sons or her husband.

Then she started to return with her daughters-in-law from the country of Moab, for she had heard in the country of Moab that the Lord had had consideration for his people and given them food. So she set out from the place where she had been living, she and her two daughters-in-law, and they went on their way to go back to the land of Judah. But Naomi said to her two daughters-in-law, "Go back each of you to your mother's house. May the Lord deal kindly with you, as you have dealt with the dead and with me. The Lord grant that you may find security, each of you in the house of your husband." Then she kissed them, and they wept aloud. They said to her, "No, we will return with you to your people." But Naomi said, "Turn back, my daughters, why

will you go with me? Do I still have sons in my womb that they may become your husbands? Turn back, my daughters, go your way, for I am too old to have a husband. Even if I thought there was hope for me, even if I should have a husband tonight and bear sons, would you then wait until they were grown? Would you then refrain from marrying? No, my daughters, it has been far more bitter for me than for you, because the hand of the LORD has turned against me." Then they wept aloud again. Orpah kissed her mother-in-law, but Ruth clung to her.

So she said, "See, your sister-in-law has gone back to her people and to her gods; return after your sister-in-law." But Ruth said,

"Do not press me to leave you
  or to turn back from following you!
Where you go, I will go;
  where you lodge, I will lodge;
your people shall be my people,
  and your God my God.
Where you die, I will die—
  there will I be buried.
May the LORD do thus and so to me,
  and more as well,
if even death parts me from you!"

When Naomi saw that she was determined to go with her, she said no more to her.

So the two of them went on until they came to Bethlehem. When they came to Bethlehem, the whole town was stirred because of them; and the women said, "Is this Naomi?" (Ruth 1:1–19)

The Loyal Daughter-In-Law

The book of Ruth is the beautiful story of Ruth's willingness to go to remarkable lengths to stand by her mother-in-law. Although Ruth would have been more comfortable in familiar surroundings, speaking her own language, and following the customs she grew up with, she chose to venture to a strange land. As a poor, widowed foreigner, Ruth would have no status in her new home. No one—not even Naomi—would have condemned Ruth for returning to her home and family, as Orpah did. Ruth's decision to accompany Naomi to Israel was just the beginning of her loyalty.

Once in Bethlehem, Ruth's devotion continued to show itself in her actions. She worked—as the needy did in that culture—gathering leftover grain in the fields of wealthy landowners. She accepted this humble and physically demanding work to feed herself and her mother-in-law, who was probably too old for manual labor.

Ruth found herself working in the field of Boaz, who, as a relative of Naomi's deceased husband, would have been responsible for taking care of her. Ruth obediently and prudently followed Naomi's instructions and presented herself as a wife for Boaz, as was proper to do according to the customs of the time. Apparently, Boaz was not a young man. When Ruth approached him seeking marriage, he praised her for not seeking a younger and presumably more attractive mate (see Ruth 3:10–11).

Ruth's quiet acts of faithfulness to her mother-in-law, which were far beyond what might have been expected from a foreigner, spoke volumes. They won Ruth the respect and admiration of Boaz and the entire town.

Ruth's story speaks of her loyalty, but also of the Divine Providence that prompted her and provided for her and Naomi. God had a plan for this foreigner. Ruth demonstrated to the Israelite community that God works through whomever he chooses—even a foreign widow

with no standing in the Israelite social order. Ruth's choices provided her and Naomi a place of security. Moreover, after marrying Boaz, Ruth gave birth to a son, Obed, who became grandfather of the great King David (see Ruth 4:13, 17).

Faithful Love

Heroic loyalty like Ruth's is called for and answered in a myriad of ways today. Caregivers stand by loved ones. Sometimes they make valiant efforts to provide for a family member's needs at home, as when Ruth labored in the fields. Other times caregivers make the equally challenging decision to enlist help, as when Ruth turned to Boaz. Families search for the best nursing care they can afford to provide for their loved ones and continue to monitor that care.

Married couples who remain faithful over the years also demonstrate heroic loyalty, whether they endured monumental financial problems, catastrophic health crises, or the mind-numbing and unglamorous challenges of day-to-day living. In fact, Ruth's speech to Naomi about going wherever she went, Naomi's people being Ruth's people, is sometimes used in wedding ceremonies to indicate a promise of loyalty in marriage.

Sometimes it takes heroic loyalty to remain true to our own values in the face of outside pressure from peer groups and society. Maybe we have honored past commitments, maybe we haven't. None of us can undo the past. With God's help, all of us can make choices that are in our best interests and those of others as we go forward.

Questions for Reflection and Discussion

1. Why do you think Ruth made the decision to leave her familiar way of life and stand by Naomi?

2. Do you think you could have made the same decision? Why or why not?

3. In spite of being a foreigner from the enemy country of Moab, Ruth's actions won the respect and admiration of the Israelite community. When in your experience have actions spoken louder than words?

4. Ruth earned the respect and admiration of an entire community, but if no one had noticed besides Naomi, would her actions have been worth it? Have you ever done anything out of loyal service, but not been rewarded or noticed for it? How did it make you feel?

CHAPTER NINE

Samuel
Great Prophet, But Still Human

The LORD said to Samuel, "How long will you grieve over Saul? I have rejected him from being king over Israel. Fill your horn with oil and set out; I will send you to Jesse the Bethlehemite, for I have provided for myself a king among his sons." Samuel said, "How can I go? If Saul hears of it, he will kill me." And the LORD said, "Take a heifer with you, and say, 'I have come to sacrifice to the LORD.' Invite Jesse to the sacrifice, and I will show you what you shall do; and you shall anoint for me the one whom I name to you." Samuel did what the LORD commanded, and came to Bethlehem. The elders of the city came to meet him trembling, and said, "Do you come peaceably?" He said, "Peaceably; I have come to sacrifice to the LORD; sanctify yourselves and come with me to the sacrifice." And he sanctified Jesse and his sons and invited them to the sacrifice.

When they came, he looked on Eliab and thought, "Surely the Lord's anointed is now before the LORD." But the LORD said to Samuel, "Do not look on his appearance or on the height of his stature, because I have rejected him; for the LORD does not see as mortals see; they look on the outward appearance, but the LORD looks on the heart." Then Jesse called Abinadab, and made him pass before Samuel. He said, "Neither has the LORD chosen this one." Then Jesse made Shammah pass by. And he said, "Neither has the LORD chosen this one." Jesse made seven of his sons pass before Samuel, and Samuel said to Jesse, "The LORD has not

chosen any of these." Samuel said to Jesse, "Are all your sons here?" And he said, "There remains yet the youngest, but he is keeping the sheep." And Samuel said to Jesse, "Send and bring him; for we will not sit down until he comes here." He sent and brought him in. Now he was ruddy, and had beautiful eyes, and was handsome. The LORD said, "Rise and anoint him; for this is the one." Then Samuel took the horn of oil, and anointed him in the presence of his brothers; and the spirit of the LORD came mightily upon David from that day forward. Samuel then set out and went to Ramah. (1 Samuel 16:1–13)

Yes!

Before his birth, Samuel's parents made the decision to dedicate him to the Lord (1 Samuel 1:11, 24–28). Samuel had no say in how he was raised. Although his early training was part of God's plan, it did not negate Samuel's free will. There comes a time when each individual has to make his or her own decision about answering God's call. Samuel said yes early on and continued to say yes throughout his life.

When the Lord first spoke to him as a young boy, Samuel mistook God's voice for that of Eli, his spiritual mentor. Eli redirected Samuel's attention to God. When questioned about what God revealed to him, Samuel answered honestly. He told Eli God planned to punish Eli's sons and descendants with destruction (see 1 Samuel 3:2–18). What courage it must have taken for the boy Samuel to risk his mentor's disapproval. Eli was the authority responsible for his well-being. Samuel risked potentially threatening consequences to speak God's truth to Eli.

In adulthood, Samuel continued to speak God's word and led the people of Israel as an honest judge and prophet. When the people wanted a king, Samuel, under God's guidance, anointed Saul, who became king and led the Israelites to victory against their enemies.

Saul's arrogance and disobedience caused God to reject Saul's continued kingship (see 1 Samuel chapters 8–15). God then instructed Samuel to anoint a new king.

Although devoted to God, Samuel was not above feeling fear at the thought of crossing Saul. Furthermore, in spite of a lifetime of service to the Lord, Samuel *still* had trouble perceiving God's will. For example, when Samuel was impressed by the physical attractiveness of each of Jesse's older sons, God had to remind Samuel not to be influenced by good looks (see 1 Samuel 16:7).

I find it reassuring that Samuel had to be reminded not to be taken in by externals. It is natural to be influenced by physical appearance. Madison Avenue and Hollywood make millions cashing in on that human tendency. It might be argued that after a lifetime of fellowship with God, Samuel would have been beyond that. He wasn't.

In fairness to Samuel, it so happened that the first king God selected, Saul, had been extremely handsome and well built (1 Samuel 9:2). Samuel might have assumed God was using the same criteria. In any event, in spite of his age and wisdom, Samuel got it wrong. God didn't hold it against him. God simply helped him regain perspective.

With heightened awareness, Samuel then discerned that each of Jesse's sons subsequently presented was not the chosen one. When the last son present was introduced, Samuel did not second-guess. He asked if there was another son. The only son left was the youngest, and he was tending sheep—not the most prestigious responsibility in the family chain of command. But Samuel, now renewed, was no longer seeing as the world sees.

When he saw David, he did see another handsome man. But Samuel now looked deeper, intuiting that David was God's choice. He obediently anointed David, the youngest son, in front of his brothers. No doubt this was an affront to the natural pecking order.

Called and Chosen

Scripture has much more to say about Samuel, but these few incidents offer much to think about. Samuel was dedicated at birth, but still needed to make his own decision to follow God. Those of us who have been brought up in a religious body from birth can take heart. We are not following God because we have no choice. There is always a choice. In fact, we face that choice many times each day.

As a boy, Samuel mistook God's voice for that of Eli, his spiritual teacher. We are called by God to share our faith in community, and we all need help to grow spiritually. But while we learn from others, it is important to remember they are human. We must not put them on a pedestal. God alone belongs in first place.

Even after a lifetime of serving God, Samuel still mistook God's intention while discerning which of Jesse's sons to anoint. Learning to follow God's will is a never-ending process. One of the great Old Testament prophets got it wrong after years of following God's way. So we don't have to be discouraged if after years of doing our best to follow God's plan we *still* get it wrong sometimes. God can always lead us back.

Samuel's life reassures us that dedication does not mean perfection and that imperfection does not mean ineffectiveness in serving the Lord and his people.

Questions for Reflection and Discussion

1. Samuel was raised in a faith-filled environment but still had to make his own decision to continue following God. What is your earliest recollection of being in relationship with God independent of family or community?

2. As a boy, Samuel mistook God's voice for the voice of his spiritual mentor, Eli. It is sometimes easy to confuse the message with the messenger. What are the pitfalls in placing another human being on a spiritual pedestal?

3. Samuel was intimidated at the thought of crossing Saul, but brought his fear to God. Have you ever poured out your fears to God in prayer? What happened? Are you comfortable sharing your honest feelings with God? Why or why not?

4. Despite years of dedication to God, upon seeing Jesse's oldest son, Samuel was initially taken in by his good looks. Name some superficialities that people admire today. Which of these do you most easily fall prey to? What can help provide perspective?

CHAPTER TEN

Mephibosheth
Man of Circumstance

Saul's son Jonathan had a son who was crippled in his feet. He was five years old when the news about Saul and Jonathan came from Jezreel. His nurse picked him up and fled; and, in her haste to flee, it happened that he fell and became lame. His name was Mephibosheth....

David asked, "Is there still anyone left of the house of Saul to whom I may show kindness for Jonathan's sake?" Now there was a servant of the house of Saul whose name was Ziba, and he was summoned to David. The king said to him, "Are you Ziba?" And he said, "At your service!" The king said, "Is there anyone remaining of the house of Saul to whom I may show the kindness of God?" Ziba said to the king, "There remains a son of Jonathan; he is crippled in his feet." The king said to him, "Where is he?" Ziba said to the king, "He is in the house of Machir son of Ammiel, at Lo-debar." Then King David sent and brought him from the house of Machir son of Ammiel, at Lo-debar. Mephibosheth son of Jonathan son of Saul came to David, and fell on his face and did obeisance. David said, "Mephibosheth!" He answered, "I am your servant." David said to him, "Do not be afraid, for I will show you kindness for the sake of your father Jonathan; I will restore to you all the land of your grandfather Saul, and you yourself shall eat at my table always." He did obeisance and said, "What is your servant, that you should look upon a dead dog such as I am?"...

Then the king summoned Saul's servant Ziba, and said to him, "All that belonged to Saul and to all his house I have given to your master's grandson. You and your sons and your servants shall till the land for him, and shall bring in the produce, so that your master's grandson may have food to eat; but your master's grandson Mephibosheth shall always eat at my table." Now Ziba had fifteen sons and twenty servants.

Then Ziba said to the king, "According to all that my lord the king commands his servant, so your servant will do." Mephibosheth ate at David's table, like one of the king's sons. Mephibosheth had a young son whose name was Mica. And all who lived in Ziba's house became Mephibosheth's servants. Mephibosheth lived in Jerusalem, for he always ate at the king's table. Now he was lame in both his feet. (2 Samuel 4:4; 9:1–13)

Enemy or Loyal Friend?

Saul viewed David as his mortal enemy and fought against him, seeking his death. In spite of this, the deep friendship between Saul's son Jonathan and David remained unbroken. Saul and Jonathan both died in battle. After David became king of Israel and Judah, he did not forget his love for Jonathan (see 1 Samuel 18–20). David honored his promise to show kindness to Jonathan's family. Jonathan's son Mephibosheth had been crippled when his nurse dropped him while trying to protect him from Saul's enemies, presumably including David.

Mephibosheth would have been safe under David's protection. It is unfortunate that he remained hidden from David for so long. By the time David brought Mephibosheth into his presence, Mephibosheth was a grown man with a child of his own. In David's presence, Mephibosheth initially referred to himself as a dog—and a dead one,

at that. This doesn't sound like false humility to me; it sounds like the self-perception of someone raised hiding in the shadows. He had no say about becoming crippled. He had to make the best of learning to deal with unfortunate circumstances and, apparently, he did.

Nevertheless, David had only love for Mephibosheth. When David finally paid the inheritance to Mephibosheth for the sake of his friend Jonathan, I imagine Mephibosheth might have been ill at ease. He wasn't used to the richness of life in the king's palace. Mephibosheth did nothing to earn the land, the servants, or the free ticket to lifetime meals in a palace.

What did it feel like to sit at the table and take his meals with David and his companions? I once heard Christian speaker Malcolm Smith raise that question and it is a question worth pondering. How awkward was it for Mephibosheth to receive lavish generosity from someone he grew up believing was his enemy?

Perhaps years of living in the shadows gave Mephibosheth valuable lessons in humility. When good fortune came his way, he could then appreciate it as a blessing rather than something that was his due. He could have resented the long time it took in coming, but Scripture gives no indication of this. Gratitude enhances our enjoyment of blessings.

Happiness and Sorrow

This story reminds me that it isn't always easy to accept good things when we have become accustomed to hard times. What is familiar becomes comfortable—even when it's painful at times. Part of the challenge of leaving an abusive relationship or employment situation can be risking the known discomfort for the unknown.

My own experience has taught me that change—even a turn of events for the good—can be intimidating. But God works in all circumstances. His will for us doesn't always mean hardship and sacrifice. Yes, we need to learn to accept when hard times come, drawing

nearer to him for the strength to get through them. But good times come too.

Jesus didn't refuse a good time when it came his way. In fact, he was accused of being a glutton and drunkard (see Luke 7:34). Enjoying our blessings and sharing happy times with others is healthy. However, the danger comes if we allow complacency to set in. When we take good times for granted and expect things to always run smoothly, our unrealistic expectations set us up for rude awakenings. Life seems to be a mixture of blessings and challenges.

In Luke's account of the Beatitudes, Jesus assures those who weep that they will laugh again, but also warns those who laugh that they will weep (see Luke 6:21, 25). Despite this parallel warning and blessing, I don't believe Jesus was threatening us with payback for experiencing joy. After all, joy is one of the fruits of the Holy Spirit (see Galatians 5:22). Is it possible that Jesus was warning us—at least in part—against complacency?

Mephibosheth's story demonstrates that the way things are at any point in time is not they way they will always be. Jesus embraced his times of joy and his times of sorrow. As did Mephibosheth. As we are invited to do. Whatever we are experiencing, whether to our liking or not, it all can be used for good for those who love the Lord.

Questions for Reflection and Discussion

1. The nurse caring for Mephibosheth incorrectly thought David was out to harm her charge. Throughout his early life, Mephibosheth was probably told that David was his enemy. Have you ever had misconceptions about other people's motives? How did the situation get resolved?

2. Do you see any parallels between Mephibosheth's experience and that of people who have the impression God is out to get them?

3. In attempting to protect Mephibosheth, the nurse actually did more damage, albeit inadvertently. When has trying to avoid a problem caused additional problems for you or those around you? What can be learned from this?

4. In spite of being crippled and being raised in hiding, Mephibosheth got on with his life and went on to marry and have a child. How have you been able to get on with your life in the face of adversity?

5. After one encounter with David, Mephibosheth's circumstances drastically changed for the better. What do you see as the biggest challenge in accepting a change for the good?

6. How can gratitude help us handle both blessings and misfortunes?

CHAPTER ELEVEN

Naaman
Arrogant Conqueror

Naaman, commander of the army of the king of Aram, was a great man and in high favor with his master, because by him the Lord had given victory to Aram. The man, though a mighty warrior, suffered from leprosy. Now the Arameans on one of their raids had taken a young girl captive from the land of Israel, and she served Naaman's wife. She said to her mistress, "If only my lord were with the prophet who is in Samaria! He would cure him of his leprosy." So Naaman went in and told his lord just what the girl from the land of Israel had said. And the king of Aram said, "Go then, and I will send along a letter to the king of Israel."

He went, taking with him ten talents of silver, six thousand shekels of gold, and ten sets of garments....

So Naaman came with his horses and chariots, and halted at the entrance of Elisha's house. Elisha sent a messenger to him, saying, "Go, wash in the Jordan seven times, and your flesh shall be restored and you shall be clean." But Naaman became angry and went away, saying, "I thought that for me he would surely come out, and stand and call on the name of the Lord his God, and would wave his hand over the spot, and cure the leprosy! Are not Abana and Pharpar, the rivers of Damascus, better than all the waters of Israel? Could I not wash in them, and be clean?" He turned and went away in a rage. But his servants approached and said to him, "Father, if the prophet had commanded you to do something difficult, would you not have done it? How much more, when all he

said to you was, 'Wash, and be clean'?" So he went down and immersed himself seven times in the Jordan, according to the word of the man of God; his flesh was restored like the flesh of a young boy, and he was clean.

Then he returned to the man of God, he and all his company; he came and stood before him and said, "Now I know that there is no God in all the earth except in Israel; please accept a present from your servant." But he said, "As the LORD lives, whom I serve, I will accept nothing!" He urged him to accept, but he refused. Then Naaman said, "If not, please let two mule-loads of earth be given to your servant; for your servant will no longer offer burnt offering or sacrifice to any god except the LORD. But may the LORD pardon your servant on one count: when my master goes into the house of Rimmon to worship there, leaning on my arm, and I bow down in the house of Rimmon, when I do bow down in the house of Rimmon, may the LORD pardon your servant on this one count." He said to him, "Go in peace." (2 Kings 5:1–5, 9–19)

Victorious Soldier

Naaman was a victorious soldier. He had wealth, power, and friends in high places. Picture his cavalcade—lackeys at his beck and call and horses hauling gold, silver, and precious gifts for him. What a contrast to the prophet Elisha's humble home in the conquered land of Israel! Yet Elisha didn't even bother to come to the door. Naaman's pride was wounded at not being seen in person by the prophet.

It is easy to sit back in judgment, listening to the arrogant tirade against Elisha's instructions. But how could Naaman not be arrogant? He was used to the finer things in life. He was used to being respected and obeyed. People probably begged Naaman for favors, not the other

way around. His entire life taught him to value his own position and achievements. He failed to see, as we are told in 2 Kings 5:1 that it was the Lord who had given him victory. Naaman had been gifted by the Lord, but remained clueless until brought to his knees by his dreaded skin disease.

How humbling it must have been for him to go to a land he had already conquered and ask for help. I suspect he attempted to hang on to his dignity by the impressive parade he, his men, and his gifts made in arriving at Elisha's door. Perhaps he hoped to demonstrate his worthiness to be healed or prove himself Elisha's equal. Elisha was unimpressed. No wonder Naaman balked. It isn't easy to ask for help. Furthermore, it's hard enough to obey a superior, let alone someone you look down on.

It took Naaman's servants to point out how self-defeating his attitude was. Servants have more practice at obeying others through enlightened self-interest. Naaman didn't need a complete change of heart at first. All he needed was the willingness to take the action. Luckily for him, he brought his body to the river. His action, no matter how reluctant or resentful his heart may have felt, was sufficient to lead him to healing. Once he experienced physical healing, his attitude changed of its own accord.

Naaman returned to Elisha convinced that the only true God was the God of Israel (see 2 Kings 5:15). In gratitude, he offered Elisha a thank-you gift, but Elisha firmly refused to accept it (see 2 Kings 5:15–17) Had Elisha accepted payment that might have jeopardized Naaman's newfound sense of having been given something freely. If he reciprocated by paying for his healing, Naaman might have again felt he was indebted to no man or God for his blessings.

Instead, Naaman asked for something further. He wanted two "mule-loads" of earth to take home because it was believed that one could worship God only on his home territory. Naaman, returning

home, wanted to take God's "turf" with him. He wanted to continue to worship the One he had discovered to be the only true God.

Naaman went home with a lot more than a body freed of a dreaded skin disease and two mule-loads of earth. He went home healed of the dreaded soul-sickness of arrogance that eats at a person's relationship with God, with others, and even with a sense of his own true self. Naaman traded pride in his accomplishments for the true self-esteem that comes from knowing we are worthy because our Creator loved us into existence. This puts us on equal footing with all our fellow humans, regardless of talents and worldly accomplishments (or lack thereof).

A Process of Conversion

Most of us have balked at doing things in a way that felt demeaning or just contrary to our will. Wanting our way over someone else's way (even if that someone else is God) can mean arrogantly thinking our way is best. Most of us have also felt uncomfortable asking for help. It stings our pride. It often feels easier to be the giver. When we receive without reciprocating, it's uncomfortable. We feel beholden. Most of us don't find it easy to depend on others, unless forced to do so by dire straits. But we are all indebted to God for every breath we take. What do any of us have that is not a gift from God? Being reminded of this keeps us humble in a healthy way.

The imperfection of our growth can also be humbling. Naaman's experience brought him back home a changed man, but not so changed that he was willing to defy his king. Naaman acknowledged that he would accompany his king to the temple of the Syrian god Rimmon, while understanding that this god was not real. Naaman was not hedging his bets. Any external compliance he demonstrated in acquiescence to his king would not shake Naaman's faith in the true God or his trust in God's mercy.

There was an indelible mark on Naaman's soul that couldn't help but be noticed by others back home. His change of heart, as well as his change in body, would be a powerful witness to the power of God. Maybe that is why Elisha, upon hearing his confession, sends Naaman off in peace.

Our spiritual journey is an ongoing process. Whether or not our faith experience is marked by dramatic turning points, there is always room for growth. Like Naaman, we can go forward in peace. God gives us all we need to continue growing in faith as we do our imperfect best to act on what we have already been given.

Questions for Reflection and Discussion

1. Naaman wanted—or at least expected—to merit and somehow reciprocate the help he hoped to receive. When have you received assistance with no strings attached? What was that like?

2. Think of a time when you freely offered assistance to someone who was not in a position to repay you. How did that person respond? What was that experience like for you?

3. Which is more comfortable for you: offering to help others or asking for help for yourself? Why? How might this awareness influence your interactions with others?

4. Which of God's free gifts are you most grateful for today?

[• CHAPTER TWELVE •]

Nehemiah
Humble Exile

The words of Nehemiah son of Hacaliah. In the month of Chislev, in the twentieth year, while I was in Susa the capital, one of my brothers, Hanani, came with certain men from Judah; and I asked them about the Jews that survived, those who had escaped the captivity, and about Jerusalem. They replied, "The survivors there in the province who escaped captivity are in great trouble and shame; the wall of Jerusalem is broken down, and its gates have been destroyed by fire."

When I heard these words I sat down and wept, and mourned for days, fasting and praying before the God of heaven. I said, "O LORD God of heaven, the great and awesome God who keeps covenant and steadfast love with those who love him and keep his commandments; let your ear be attentive and your eyes open to hear the prayer of your servant that I now pray before you day and night for your servants, the people of Israel, confessing the sins of the people of Israel, which we have sinned against you. Both I and my family have sinned. We have offended you deeply, failing to keep the commandments, the statutes, and the ordinances that you commanded your servant Moses. Remember the word that you commanded your servant Moses, 'If you are unfaithful, I will scatter you among the peoples; but if you return to me and keep my commandments and do them, though your outcasts are under the farthest skies, I will gather them from there and bring them to the place at which I have chosen to establish my name.' They are your servants

and your people, whom you redeemed by your great power and your strong hand. O Lord, let your ear be attentive to the prayer of your servant, and to the prayer of your servants who delight in revering your name. Give success to your servant today, and grant him mercy in the sight of this man!"

At the time, I was cupbearer to the king.

In the month of Nisan, in the twentieth year of King Artaxerxes, when wine was served him, I carried the wine and gave it to the king. Now, I had never been sad in his presence before. So the king said to me, "Why is your face sad, since you are not sick? This can only be sadness of the heart." Then I was very much afraid. I said to the king, "May the king live forever! Why should my face not be sad, when the city, the place of my ancestors' graves, lies waste, and its gates have been destroyed by fire?" Then the king said to me, "What do you request?" So I prayed to the God of heaven. Then I said to the king, "If it pleases the king, and if your servant has found favor with you, I ask that you send me to Judah, to the city of my ancestors' graves, so that I may rebuild it." The king said to me (the queen also was sitting beside him), "How long will you be gone, and when will you return?" So it pleased the king to send me, and I set him a date. (Nehemiah 1:1—2:1–6)

The Steward

Nehemiah, a wine steward, ended up as governor of Judah. He organized the rebuilding of the wall of Jerusalem, overcame opposition, reinstituted worship in the Temple, and renewed the proclamation of and practice of the faith. Not bad for a captive who had lived in exile waiting on his captor for who knows how long. How did he do it?

The book of Nehemiah does not describe fantastic visions, or

dramatic miracles. What is demonstrated, over and over again, is Nehemiah's unassuming faith and practical application of it. He was living away from his homeland and in a subservient position. When he heard news that his beloved Jerusalem was in desperate straits, he was deeply saddened. One obvious response would have been resentment.

Many people rail against God in their grief. Nehemiah humbly accepted responsibility along with his people for having brought the exile upon themselves through their own disobedience. However, he did not waste time wallowing in guilt or self-effacing claims of unworthiness. Nehemiah's faith prompted him to hope that God would rescue him and his people—not because of their own merit, but because of God's power and mercy.

Nehemiah's faith didn't waiver when his prayer seemed unanswered. We are told that it was the month of Nisan (four months after his original prayer) when the emperor took notice of Nehemiah's sadness. He had seen Artaxerxes every day at dinner when he brought him his wine, but Nehemiah had never asserted himself. He quietly went about his responsibilities. In God's time, Artaxerxes noticed Nehemiah's unhappiness. When asked, Nehemiah didn't jump in with an immediate response. He took a moment to pray to God before responding. How many of us can say we've done the same? How many of us have bungled opportunities in our anxiousness to solve a problem, by forgetting to pause and connect with God's will instead of forging ahead on our own initiative?

Nehemiah is an example of patience, prudence, and humility. He didn't resent his humble station as wine steward. He didn't give in to impatience or lose faith when his prayer seemed unanswered. He quietly fulfilled his daily obligations. The faithful performance of his duties and his lack of presumption may have inspired Artaxerxes to trust this prudent man to govern Jerusalem.

But Nehemiah's lack of presumption did not signal lack of courage. When challenged and ridiculed by those who opposed him in Jerusalem, he did not lose heart or quit (see Nehemiah 4:1–6). When work on the city wall was threatened by attack, he prudently had half the men stand guard as the other half worked on the wall (see 4:11–21). When the poor complained of their oppression, Nehemiah took on the Jewish leaders who were oppressing their own people (see 5:1–13). His opponents devised a plot to trick him into protecting himself from a personal threat. Nehemiah did not act out of cowardice. He refused to take the bait (see 6:1–14).

He also demonstrated wisdom in restoring order to the city. When all the physical work was completed, Nehemiah methodically checked available records, taking a type of census to organize and facilitate administrative operations. Temple duties were assigned and methods of worship were restored. He called the people together so the law could be read to them. They confessed their sins, and renewed their agreement to live under God's law (see chapters 7—10).

Sticking to the Plan

Step by step, Nehemiah handled the events and challenges that came along. By unremarkable means he achieved remarkable things, because he relied on God, and kept on taking the next right action to deal with the matter at hand.

Nehemiah's story reminds us that we can also serve in important but unspectacular ways. When Nehemiah heard the sad news about his beloved homeland, he wept and prayed. There were bolder options. Another man might have rebelled, escaped, or at least taken the initiative to approach the emperor on Jerusalem's behalf. Instead, Nehemiah continued to serve quietly.

It's reassuring to see God work through Nehemiah. Not all of us have an assertive personality. Nehemiah's story demonstrates that God has plans for us, too. We can faithfully perform the tasks at hand.

When opportunities present themselves, we can accept the responsibilities that come our way.

If we find ourselves in a negative situation, we can trust that God has already provided what we need to fulfill our role. Like Nehemiah, we can keep turning to God and then keep taking the next right step. We can be who we are. God can use us when we are true to our own nature.

Questions for Reflection and Discussion

1. Immediately after hearing of Jerusalem's sad state, Nehemiah took no overt action. He wept, mourned, prayed, and did not eat for several days. How do you think these actions contributed to the turn of events that led to the rebuilding of Jerusalem?

2. Four months after Nehemiah started mourning, the emperor addressed Nehemiah's sadness. Although startled, Nehemiah responded with heartfelt honesty. Have circumstances ever taken you by surprise? Without the opportunity to rehearse your reaction, did you find that you responded from the heart? How did it turn out?

3. When asked what he wanted, Nehemiah took time to pray to the God of heaven before answering. How can connecting with God influence what you want or think you want?

4. Nehemiah longed for a solution to Jerusalem's plight. When asked, he volunteered to take an active part in the solution. What situation would you like to see changed for the better? How can you participate in the solution?

CHAPTER THIRTEEN

Esther
Orphan Queen

Then the king's servants who attended him said, "Let beautiful young virgins be sought out for the king. And let the king
appoint commissioners in all the provinces of his kingdom to
gather all the beautiful young virgins to the harem in the citadel of Susa under custody of Hegai, the king's eunuch, who
is in charge of the women; let their cosmetic treatments be
given them. And let the girl who pleases the king be queen
instead of Vashti." This pleased the king, and he did so.

Now there was a Jew in the citadel of Susa whose name was
Mordecai son of Jair son of Shimei son of Kish, a Benjaminite.
Kish had been carried away from Jerusalem among the cap-
tives carried away with King Jeconiah of Judah, whom King
Nebuchadnezzar of Babylon had carried away. Mordecai had
brought up Hadassah, that is Esther, his cousin, for she had
neither father nor mother; the girl was fair and beautiful, and
when her father and her mother died, Mordecai adopted her
as his own daughter. So when the king's order and his edict
were proclaimed, and when many young women were gathered in the citadel of Susa in custody of Hegai, Esther also
was taken into the king's palace and put in custody of Hegai,
who had charge of the women. The girl pleased him and
won his favor, and he quickly provided her with her cosmetic
treatments and her portion of food, and with seven chosen
maids from the king's palace, and advanced her and her
maids to the best place in the harem. Esther did not reveal
her people or kindred, for Mordecai had charged her not to
tell. Every day Mordecai would walk around in front of the

court of the harem, to learn how Esther was and how she fared.

The turn came for each girl to go in to King Ahasuerus, after being twelve months under the regulations for the women, since this was the regular period of their cosmetic treatment, six months with oil of myrrh and six months with perfumes and cosmetics for women.…

When the turn came for Esther daughter of Abihail the uncle of Mordecai, who had adopted her as his own daughter, to go in to the king, she asked for nothing except what Hegai the king's eunuch, who had charge of the women, advised. Now Esther was admired by all who saw her. When Esther was taken to King Ahasuerus in his royal palace in the tenth month, which is the month of Tebeth, in the seventh year of his reign, the king loved Esther more than all the other women; of all the virgins she won his favor and devotion, so that he set the royal crown on her head and made her queen instead of Vashti. (Esther 2:2–12, 15–17)

The Pampered Girl

Scripture makes it sound like Esther had it made. Despite being an orphan, she was raised by a loving relative who treated her as his own daughter. Because of her beauty, she was taken to the harem, where massages, beauty treatments, and handmaidens were the order of the day. She ultimately married King Ahasuerus and was made queen. Who would have guessed that God would call someone to serve him by spending time in a beauty spa? By God's plan, Esther became queen, not only for her own good fortune, but also for the good of all Jews through out the kingdom.

Esther's inner beauty must have surpassed her physical beauty. In beautiful humility, she obeyed her guardian, Mordecai, and did not let it be known in the harem that she was Jewish.

Esther's beautiful nature is further revealed since she won the favor of the head eunuch, Hagai. He was surrounded by gorgeous women in the harem every day, but favored Esther. No doubt Hagai found her as cooperative as Mordecai had. Her ability to follow instructions made her easy to get along with. Although cooperative, Esther was not servile and did not sacrifice her inner core of belief (see Esther C 14:15–18).

The book of Esther describes how Haman, the king's right-hand man, was bound to destroy the Jews in general and Mordecai in particular. Mordecai informed her of the imminent threat Haman's plan presented to all Jews, including Esther. Although Mordecai initially had ordered her not to reveal herself as a Jew, the time had come. He urged her to intervene, speculating that she may have been made queen for just "such a time as this" (Esther 4:14).

My heart goes out to Esther. Despite being queen, as a woman in the king's harem, Esther was still in a fairly powerless position. She had to feel torn between concern for her people, and the reality that interceding for them meant danger to herself. Anyone presuming to approach the king without being summoned risked death. Obedient as always, Esther asked Mordecai to call a vigil in the Jewish community for three days, while she and her maids fasted and prayed in the harem (see Esther 4:11, 15–16). The Greek translation of the book of Esther describes her taking off the luxurious trappings of beauty while she fasted and prayed to God, humbly asking for courage and the right words (see Esther C 14:1–19).

After three days, she risked death and entered the king's presence. Esther's loveliness won the king's favor. I can imagine her heart pounding as she entered his chambers. (Having courage does not mean feeling no fear.)

Esther invited the king, along with Haman, to a banquet. At a second banquet the following night, the king asked what she wanted.

She answered by requesting that she and her people be allowed to live (see Esther 7:3). Who could deny a request like that? Haman and his plan to destroy the Jews both meet their end.

Who would have thought that God would use a gorgeous, soft-spoken girl who had lived a sheltered life to save a whole nation? Esther was easy to get along with. She respected others: her guardian Mordecai, the eunuch in charge of the harem, and her husband, the king. Although compliant, she was not a doormat. She maintained her integrity by following her beliefs in the harem. Ultimately, Esther stood up for herself and those she cared about, but in a prudent and respectful way.

This blend of meekness and courage calls to mind Jesus's admonition to his followers: if slapped, they should turn the other cheek to their opponent (Matthew 5:39). The humility of presenting another cheek for assault requires more courage and demonstrates greater self-possession than the reflexive fight-or-flight response. It implies acting out of free choice rather than reacting out of victim mentality.

A Call to Valor

Many of us will never be in positions of worldly authority. We may be kept close to home due to health or family responsibilities. Most of us are not movers and shakers. That's OK. Wherever we are, we are part of God's plan. Those of us who feel as if we can't make a difference are wrong. Esther's story is filled with encouragement for us. No matter how it may appear, we are right where we belong at this moment in time.

Those of us who feel the need to jump into action can learn from Esther's wisdom. We can take time to open ourselves to God's plan through prayer. We can fast, at least from the steady diet of media. We can also reach out for the support of others. Esther did not go it alone. Although she walked into the palace alone she was walking with the support of her entire faith community. She also took her time in

making her request known to the king. Her mission was urgent, but she didn't allow it to goad her into hasty action. I wonder how things might have turned out if she had blurted out her request to the king because she just wanted to get it over with!

There is a time for meekness and also a time for assertive action. The same Jesus who instructed us to turn the other cheek also turned over the tables of the moneychangers in the Temple and called them on their behavior (Matthew 21:12–13). God's grace and wisdom enable us to discern when to act with restraint and when to assert ourselves.

Esther's story also suggests that there is a time to allow ourselves to be nurtured. Esther allowed herself to be pampered but did not take her physical beauty and comforts as the last word. Nevertheless, if she had not indulged in the luxury of the spa treatments, Esther would not have been able to play the part God called her to play when the time came. We shouldn't be afraid to nurture ourselves with some tender loving care when it seems appropriate. It might just make us better able to serve when the time comes.

Questions for Reflection and Discussion

1. Esther was obedient and respectful without sacrificing her own values. What are the greatest challenges to acting compliantly when necessary without surrendering personal integrity? What are some ways to cope with these challenges?

2. Spending time in a beauty spa placed Esther in a position to be used by God. How can allowing yourself to be nurtured empower you to serve others? Are you comfortable taking some time to nurture yourself or allowing yourself to be nurtured? Why or why not?

3. What helps you discern when to be assertive and when to show restraint?

4. In addition to prayer, Esther fasted while preparing to risk facing the king. Think of the biggest challenge you are experiencing at this time. What do you need to fast from (activities, thought patterns) to better prepare for it? How will this fasting help you?

5. Esther asked for prayers from her community to help her face her challenge. Who makes up your prayer support network?

CHAPTER FOURTEEN

Hosea
Fool for God

When the LORD first spoke through Hosea, the LORD said to Hosea, "Go, take for yourself a wife of whoredom and have children of whoredom, for the land commits great whoredom by forsaking the LORD." So he went and took Gomer daughter of Diblaim, and she conceived and bore him a son....

The LORD said to me again, "Go, love a woman who has a lover and is an adulteress, just as the LORD loves the people of Israel, though they turn to other gods and love raisin cakes." So I bought her for fifteen shekels of silver and a homer of barley and a measure of wine. And I said to her, "You must remain as mine for many days; you shall not play the whore, you shall not have intercourse with a man, nor I with you." For the Israelites shall remain many days without king or prince, without sacrifice or pillar, without ephod or teraphim. Afterward the Israelites shall return and seek the LORD their God, and David their king; they shall come in awe to the LORD and to his goodness in the latter days....

The days of punishment have come,
   the days of recompense have come;
   Israel cries,
"The prophet is a fool,
   the man of the spirit is mad!"
Because of your great iniquity,
   your hostility is great.
The prophet is a sentinel for my God over Ephraim,

yet a fowler's snare is on all his ways,
and hostility in the house of his God.
(Hosea 1:2–3; 3:1–5; 9:7–8)

Poor Hosea!

Hosea was commissioned by God to warn the Israelites about their unfaithfulness and the painful consequences. Despite an ultimate promise of hope, it was an unpopular message. Hosea experienced the brunt of the people's rejection. Their sins made them unwilling to listen to Hosea's warning. Who wants to be challenged? Who wants to change while they are still comfortable? Besides, Hosea had married a faithless woman. No doubt the Israelites felt justified in tuning him out. What did Hosea know? He married a prostitute who was cheating on him. In spite of what the Israelites thought, by giving his love to a shameless adulteress who gave her love to other men for pleasure or profit, he was obeying God (and quite possibly following his own heart).

In Old Testament times, there were no audiovisual aids as we have today. Prophets often demonstrated the concepts God wanted to communicate by acting them out. By marrying an unfaithful prostitute, Hosea was obeying God. Hosea's obedience to God, however, lost him credibility with the public. His message was unpopular to begin with, and he showed remarkably poor judgment in selecting a wife and in giving her a second chance. He obeyed at significant cost to himself. But Hosea remained faithful to his wife and to his commission to speak God's word to the people who hated him for it.

St. Paul also risked appearing foolish in order to speak God's truth. Writing to the Corinthians, he admitted that his talk about Christ's death sounded absurd to those who were not being saved, but goes on to affirm that God's apparent foolishness exceeds human wisdom. (see 1 Corinthians 1:18, 25). With our limited human understanding,

we can never grasp God's infinitely larger plan. Therefore, we must rely on faith.

Hosea remained faithful in the face of failure, rejection, and personal heartache. His was not an easy mission, but he accepted it.

Faithful Witnessing

What does Hosea's calling have to say to us? We are called to be witnesses to God's power and love. We witness by the choices we make in dealing with our circumstances. This does not mean we are called to remain in abusive relationships. It does mean that our vocation includes learning to give more weight to what God wants for us than what public opinion dictates. It means believing in the God of second chances for those willing to amend their ways. It means accepting second chances for ourselves, and giving second chances to others.

Allowing people to walk all over us is not giving them a second chance. It is enabling them to continue their same self-centered or self-destructive patterns. I suspect that this is why Hosea took back his wife only after insisting that she endure a period of abstinence before resuming their marital relationship. Being open to reconciliation within healthy boundaries is a life-giving opportunity for each person involved. This holds true not only for marriage, but also for any relationship.

Hosea's experience is a message of hope. It reassures us that God will always take us back when we turn to him. When we do, he will see us through any consequences we may have brought on ourselves by our own poor choices. More than that, Hosea's story confirms that suffering—painful though it may be—is not without purpose. Hosea's torment was not something that belonged to him alone. With God, his personal hardship was used to benefit others.

Many of us have difficult and painful challenges in our lives. Pain without a purpose is misery. Pain with a purpose is redeeming. There is hope in seeing that our misfortunes don't have to be pointless. They

can be of some value to help someone else. When we have weathered and come through our own storms, others know our words of comfort are not given lightly.

Because we have had our own share of pain, we gain credibility with those who still suffer. We offer hope in a way that those whose lives have been untouched by pain cannot. We become living examples that heartache, broken relationships, physical pain, and grief are not insurmountable with the help of God.

Questions for Reflection and Discussion

1. Hosea spoke the truth even when it was unpopular. What helps you speak the truth in the face of ridicule or rejection?

2. When has the wisdom of God proven to be wiser than human understanding in your own life?

3. Think of a time when God was able to bring strength, help, or some other positive result to others following an unfortunate or painful event in your own life or that of someone you know. How can this experience offer hope in the face of future misfortunes?

4. Just as Hosea took back his wife after her unfaithfulness, God takes us back again and again when we wander away from him. In what ways can knowledge of his forgiveness affect your own ability to forgive yourself and others?

PART TWO
New Testament

CHAPTER FIFTEEN

Madman
Mad, but Not Hopeless

And when [Jesus] had stepped out of the boat, immediately a man out of the tombs with an unclean spirit met him. He lived among the tombs; and no one could restrain him any more, even with a chain; for he had often been restrained with shackles and chains, but the chains he wrenched apart, and the shackles he broke in pieces; and no one had the strength to subdue him. Night and day among the tombs and on the mountains he was always howling and bruising himself with stones. When he saw Jesus from a distance, he ran and bowed down before him; and he shouted at the top of his voice, "What have you to do with me, Jesus, Son of the Most High God? I adjure you by God, do not torment me." For he had said to him, "Come out of the man, you unclean spirit!" Then Jesus asked him, "What is your name?" He replied, "My name is Legion; for we are many." He begged him earnestly not to send them out of the country. Now there on the hillside a great herd of swine was feeding; and the unclean spirits begged him, "Send us into the swine; let us enter them." So he gave them permission. And the unclean spirits came out and entered the swine; and the herd, numbering about two thousand, rushed down the steep bank into the lake, and were drowned in the lake.

The swineherds ran off and told it in the city and in the country. Then people came to see what it was that had happened. They came to Jesus and saw the demoniac sitting there, clothed and in his right mind, the very man who

had had the legion; and they were afraid. Those who had seen what had happened to the demoniac and to the swine reported it. Then they began to beg Jesus to leave their neighborhood. As he was getting into the boat, the man who had been possessed by demons begged him that he might be with him. But Jesus refused, and said to him, "Go home to your friends, and tell them how much the Lord has done for you, and what mercy he has shown you." And he went away and began to proclaim in the Decapolis how much Jesus had done for him; and everyone was amazed. (Mark 5:2–20)

The Madman

I find it curious that the madman took the initiative, ran to Jesus, and then asked him, "What do you want with me?" He approached Jesus yet asked what Jesus wanted of him. He also begged Jesus not to punish him. If the man "saw Jesus from a distance" and he didn't want healing, he could have avoided Jesus, couldn't he? Yet he seemed drawn to Jesus in spite of fearing punishment. It seems like the better part of him wanted change, but dreaded what it might involve.

The man feared life without his demons, even though they caused him anguish. Nobody was able to keep the man chained up because of his physical strength. He resisted control by others, but he kept himself imprisoned. He was strong enough to go wherever he wanted. Who could stop him? Nevertheless he lived among the tombs, tormenting himself with self-destructive behavior. He screamed, cut himself, wandered aimlessly, and remained in isolation. It sounds like a pretty miserable existence.

Desperation may have given him just enough courage to approach Jesus. Maybe that's why he ran to Jesus, before he changed his mind. The man feared living without the demons because they had become familiar and were his only companions. He referred to himself as

"Legion" or "Mob" as some versions translate it. Sometimes, it certainly seems like the forces of chaos and self-destruction gang up on us. The man yearned for a better life but feared letting go of the only existence he knew. He interceded on the demons' behalf until it seemed that they were speaking for themselves. Jesus gave the evil spirits what they wanted, which led to the destruction of a herd of pigs.

The Madman and Us

The madman's experience parallels the story of recovery from addiction and other self-destructive behaviors for many of us today. Addicts often resist any attempt by others to control, influence, or interfere with their actions. Under the false hope of short-term happiness, many remain bullied by their out-of-control feelings and self-will. Isolation and self-defeating behaviors become more entrenched.

But pain can become an ally when it drives people to seek healing from a source outside of themselves and turn—however doubtfully, reluctantly, or fearfully—to God. It is easy to fear punishment for wrong choices made in the past. It is easy to fear the prospect of a future without a familiar crutch. But healing is a package deal.

Saying yes to God's healing power means letting go of self-destructive behaviors. It means turning a deaf ear to promptings that would have us obey their demands in the name of doing what we want. Step by step, the madman did what he could. By presenting himself to Jesus he honestly acknowledged his powerlessness to defeat the evil tendencies that outnumbered him.

Once he became willing to let go of the demons, he saw that he had a choice. The man dared to believe that although the demons were stronger than he was, they were not stronger than God. That left him free to remain at Jesus's feet, and made room for peace in his heart. Jesus met him there and did the rest.

Freedom Through Surrender

Loss of profit explains why the pig herders wanted Jesus to leave the territory. What about the other people? Those who came to check out the story found the man healed. He was at peace and in his right mind. Why did this threaten them? Why did they want Jesus to leave? Did they feel challenged by this example to face their own demons? Fear provides powerful motivation and is not always obvious.

When Jesus prepared to leave, the man begged to go with him. Maybe he yearned for a fresh start. But Jesus sent him back home, to bear witness to his own people of God's power and goodness. He had been transformed before their eyes. Therefore, he could witness in a way no foreigner could do. It also provided an opportunity for the man to heal the damaged relationships caused by his affliction. The man, restored to his right mind, obeyed.

Sometimes a fresh start can help us put the past behind us. A new job or change of scenery can shift our focus and enable us to change for the better, using what we've learned from past mistakes. There is a time to let bygones be bygones. But if we are slinking away, seeking a geographic cure to eliminate past regrets, we are likely to be disappointed. We take ourselves, and our memories, wherever we go. Sometimes the only way to free ourselves of past regrets is to face them and deal with them in the present. We can then change for the better what is in our power to change, and leave the rest in God's hands.

I wonder how important it might have been for the madman in the story to make amends for the damage his past behavior caused. Maybe some important relationships needed an opportunity for healing. After all, Jesus called many people to leave everything and follow him. Why not this man? Maybe in this case, the man was not so much drawn to follow Jesus, as he was anxious to run away from his past. We aren't told, so we can't know his motivations. We can't know

the motivations of anyone else, and we don't need to know. What we can do is look into our own hearts, check our own motivations, and ask what—if anything—the Lord might be calling us to do about our own past.

God can bring us out of our own turmoil—not just for our own benefit, but also to help others in a way that we could never do if we had not been through our own private hell.

Questions for Reflection and Discussion

1. Before his healing, the madman seemed to want what Jesus offered while resisting it at the same time. When have you felt drawn by and resistant to what Jesus offered you? What happened?

2. The man referred to himself as "Legion" because he felt many demons within him. Have you ever felt like the forces of negativity —discouragement, resentment, and the like—were ganging up on you? What helped you get through it?

3. In spite of seeing the madman changed for the better, the townspeople were afraid and asked Jesus to leave their territory. What do you suppose might make people feel frightened or threatened by someone else's recovery? What words of reassurance could you offer to someone threatened by another person's growth?

4. How do you know when God is inviting you to move in a new direction and when he is inviting you to grow where you're planted?

[• CHAPTER SIXTEEN •]

Anna
From Widow to Contemplative

Now there was a man in Jerusalem whose name was Simeon; this man was righteous and devout, looking forward to the consolation of Israel, and the Holy Spirit rested on him. It had been revealed to him by the Holy Spirit that he would not see death before he had seen the Lord's Messiah. Guided by the Spirit, Simeon came into the temple; and when the parents brought in the child Jesus, to do for him what was customary under the law, Simeon took him in his arms and praised God, saying,

"Master, now you are dismissing your servant in peace,
> according to your word;
for my eyes have seen your salvation,
> which you have prepared in the presence of all peoples,
a light for revelation to the Gentiles
> and for glory to your people Israel."...

There was also a prophet, Anna the daughter of Phanuel, of the tribe of Asher. She was of a great age, having lived with her husband seven years after her marriage, then as a widow to the age of eighty-four. She never left the temple but worshiped there with fasting and prayer night and day. At that moment she came, and began to praise God and to speak about the child to all who were looking for the redemption of Jerusalem. (Luke 2:25–32, 36–38)

The Young Widow

Anna didn't start out to live the life of a contemplative. She was betrothed and then married, probably at an early age, as was the

custom at that time. Perhaps as a child she imagined what her wedding day would be like. She may have daydreamed about life with her husband-to-be, and of having children of her own. Her life did seem to follow that pattern initially. She was married for seven years. She then became a widow and spent her days and nights worshiping God by fasting and praying in the Temple.

It is possible that as a young widow, Anna had opportunities to remarry but chose to remain single. Maybe her husband had left her financially secure so that she could afford to spend her time in God's praise. On the other hand, maybe she had no offers of marriage, no money at all, and fasted initially out of necessity. Living off the alms of others and God's providence, she might have learned to trust that same providence.

We are not told in Scripture, but it seems possible that she had no children. With no family of her own, I wonder if Anna sought to fill the void within her heart through a loving relationship with God. Like many others, Anna may have turned to God because she had nowhere else to turn. She had run out of resources, whether materially or emotionally, and found her answer in the love of God.

In any event, at the age of eighty-four, she persevered in following what had sustained her throughout most of her life. Her husband had been taken away. If she had children, they grew to live their own lives. Lack of status, security, and close family ties might have deepened Anna's union with the one thing that could not be taken away from her: God's love.

Seeing the Messiah
Although not the way of life she originally intended, Anna persevered. Her loss was eventually replaced with a special gift. By persistently going about her daily routine with the eyes of faith, she was privileged to see the child, the Messiah, that all of Israel had been awaiting for generations.

It is quite possible that the religious officials in the Temple looked on Anna with disdain. The Lord had condemned the religious leaders for taking advantage of widows (Mark 12:38–40). Maybe Anna was one of those widows. If so, her testimony about the baby Jesus, along with Simeon's, was all the more remarkable.

God introduced his Chosen One through the truly dedicated upholders of the Jewish faith, not the religious leaders. As often happened throughout Christ's ministry, the respected leaders of the religious community missed the significance of his presence. Jesus later rejoiced in the opportunity this presented to all sincere believers—educated or not—when he gave thanks to the Father for revealing to the unlearned what was hidden from the wise and intelligent (see Matthew 11:25).

The task of spreading the Good News fell to the humble faithful who were open to receive it. Anna took up the task with gratitude and enthusiasm, thanking God and speaking about the child to all who would listen, that is, those with open hearts. Certainly not the religious leaders who would not have been particularly anxious for anything to shake up the status quo!

Those seeking God and longing for change would listen to Anna. She would be there to tell them, in the Temple where she had spent most of her life. Her lifetime of prayer in the Temple didn't need to change in order for her to spread the good news. She was where she needed to be.

Living God's Message

Life doesn't always turn out the way we plan. Accepting circumstances beyond our control frees us to focus on the opportunities we find in our reality. Not all of us are called to shout our message from the rooftops. Those of us called to a quiet, reflective lifestyle have an important place in God's plan, just as those of us who are called to serve more actively. There is room for all in God's kingdom.

People can be drawn to a contemplative lifestyle by vocation, nature, or circumstance. There are religious orders dedicated to prayer and silent reflection. Some people, like the hermits of times past, seem to seek solitude apart from religious communities. Others find themselves isolated or homebound, if only temporarily, by circumstances such as physical challenges, or because they care for others with special needs.

My own health problems have left me home for months at a time more than once in my life. I've also found myself isolated in the middle of the night by insomnia. By God's grace, I've been able to use these times alone for increased spiritual reading and prayer. Though initially forced by circumstances, I came to appreciate, more often than not, these opportunities for time apart with God.

Even those of us with busy lifestyles do well to interrupt our demanding schedules periodically for times of rest and reflection. Whether we accept opportunities for quiet prayer or create our own, these times renew us. More than that, they can equip us, like Anna, to share the good news with those still waiting to be set free.

Questions for Reflection and Discussion

1. Widowed after seven years of marriage, Anna spent her life worshiping God in the Temple. When have you experienced, or observed in others, abrupt and unplanned changes in circumstances? What opportunities for spiritual growth were present in those times?

2. Anna worshiped God "day and night." What are some ways to worship God while going about your daily activities?

3. What opportunities for contemplation can you find in your current lifestyle?

4. Anna spoke about the Christ child to all who were waiting for God to set Jerusalem free. Can you think of anyone still waiting to be set free? How can you share the good news with them?

CHAPTER SEVENTEEN

Martha
Worrier, but Faithful Witness

Now as they went on their way, he entered a certain village, where a woman named Martha welcomed him into her home. She had a sister named Mary, who sat at the Lord's feet and listened to what he was saying. But Martha was distracted by her many tasks; so she came to him and asked, "Lord, do you not care that my sister has left me to do all the work by myself? Tell her then to help me." But the Lord answered her, "Martha, Martha, you are worried and distracted by many things; there is need of only one thing. Mary has chosen the better part, which will not be taken away from her." (Luke 10:38-42)

When Jesus arrived, he found that Lazarus had already been in the tomb four days. Now Bethany was near Jerusalem, some two miles away, and many of the Jews had come to Martha and Mary to console them about their brother. When Martha heard that Jesus was coming, she went and met him, while Mary stayed at home. Martha said to Jesus, "Lord, if you had been here, my brother would not have died. But even now I know that God will give you whatever you ask of him." Jesus said to her, "Your brother will rise again." Martha said to him, "I know that he will rise again in the resurrection on the last day." Jesus said to her, "I am the resurrection and the life. Those who believe in me, even though they die, will live, and everyone who lives and believes in me will never die. Do you believe this?" She said to him, "Yes,

Lord, I believe that you are the Messiah, the Son of God, the
one coming into the world." (John 11:17–27)

The Hustler and Bustler
Martha couldn't sit still. While mourning her brother's death, she still
took the initiative to go meet Jesus as soon as she heard he was on his
way. Her sister, Mary, stayed home and only ventured out after Jesus
sent for her. It's not surprising. Mary was the one who was content
to sit at Jesus's feet during his earlier visit to their home. By contrast,
Martha hustled and bustled, busy with all the work involved in enter-
taining a guest—and such a special guest as Jesus.

Those of us who are practical and detail-oriented probably sym-
pathize with Martha. As anyone who has ever had company knows,
there is quite a bit of work involved in preparation and clean up. *These
dishes aren't going to wash themselves! If I don't do it, who will?* Thoughts
like these come easily when there's a lot to do and too few hands to do
it. But what we may not realize is that our itineraries are sometimes
unrealistic or filled with unnecessary activity.

Jesus didn't say, "Martha, Martha, stop being a hard worker." He
said she was "worried and distracted by many things." Anxiety fueled
by perfectionism may have driven Martha to needless busywork.
Could her anxiousness, not her activity level, have been the problem?

Martha's faith is not in question. Her affirmation of faith in Jesus as
the Messiah, the Son of God, does not waiver—even in the pain and
confusion following her brother's death. Bitter disillusionment would
have been understandable. Jesus healed so many others, yet failed
to be there in time to heal his good friend, Lazarus. Nevertheless,
Martha affirmed her faith in Jesus before she witnessed him raise her
brother from death.

Jesus loved Martha as well as Mary and their brother Lazarus (see
John 11:5). When he said, "Martha, Martha," it's easy to picture him

gently shaking his head with loving concern. (I sometimes imagine him shaking his head at my foolish and self-defeating behavior, too.) As he invited Martha, Jesus invites the rest of us to let go of habits that take on a life of their own.

Finding Balance

Compulsive activity can lure us into setting standards we can't meet without distorting the balance in our lives. We lose perspective. When we try to impose those standards on others it creates tension. Focused on her goal, I suspect Martha did everything she could to get Mary to help her before appealing to someone with more clout—Jesus.

Some people are laid back. Others are more active. Although habits and attitudes can be unlearned and modified, I see Jesus respecting individual differences. While gently inviting Martha to let go of her self-imposed burden, he firmly refused to have that inclination imposed on her sister.

Some of us may find we have both Martha and Mary tendencies within us. While basking in Scripture and contemplating the eternal are unquestionably rewarding, they are not passports to procrastination or inertia. There are tasks that need to be done in the real world. On the other hand, the times we feel most driven are the times we most need—and are least-inclined—to pause and breathe in the presence of the Holy Spirit. When we are tired or frantic it's hard to see clearly what really needs to be done now and what can be postponed until tomorrow—or even indefinitely.

"The LORD is my shepherd, I shall not want" (Psalm 23:1). Or we might say, "The Lord is my shepherd; I have everything I need" (as the *Good News* translation renders it). Indeed, everything we need includes the time and energy to do what God has in mind for us to do on any given day. A shepherd's staff has a curve at one end to gently pull back those who wander or even scurry away from the right path. The staff also has a blunt end for moving along those who need

prodding. Balance and freedom from obsessive worry is the goal. May we find that balance by God's grace.

Questions for Reflection and Discussion

1. What are some of the things that may have been driving Martha to be "worried and troubled over so many things"?

2. What might have helped her to let go of her need to act on her busyness? What might help you?

3. If, like Martha, you truly believe that Jesus is the Messiah, the Son of God, how does that affect your own "to do" lists?

4. What can you do to slow down when the "Martha" part of your personality nags you?

5. How can you balance being occupied with practical matters and taking time for quiet reflection?

CHAPTER EIGHTEEN

Andrew
Good Brother

The next day John again was standing with two of his disciples, and as he watched Jesus walk by, he exclaimed, "Look, here is the Lamb of God!" The two disciples heard him say this, and they followed Jesus. When Jesus turned and saw them following, he said to them, "What are you looking for?" They said to him, "Rabbi" (which translated means Teacher), "where are you staying?" He said to them, "Come and see." They came and saw where he was staying, and they remained with him that day. It was about four o'clock in the afternoon. One of the two who heard John speak and followed him was Andrew, Simon Peter's brother. He first found his brother Simon and said to him, "We have found the Messiah" (which is translated Anointed). He brought Simon to Jesus, who looked at him and said, "You are Simon son of John. You are to be called Cephas" (which is translated Peter). (John 1:35–42)

"But I Saw Him First!"

If Andrew was anything like me, that might have been his first thought when Jesus nicknamed Andrew's brother "the Rock." After taking the initiative to follow Jesus, Andrew didn't cling to exclusivity. He wanted to share what he found. He looked for his brother Simon Peter and introduced him to Jesus—only to have Jesus pick that brother to be the "rock" on which Jesus would build his Church.

Jesus also promised to give Peter the "keys of the kingdom of heaven" (Matthew 16:18–19). Imagine how Andrew might have

reacted. "Humph. Some thanks I get for listening to John the Baptist, following Jesus, and then introducing you to him, Simon Peter. You get the limelight and I'm in the shadows." If that thought crossed Andrew's mind, I would understand perfectly.

But the Gospels never tell us that Andrew had any resentment or illusions of grandeur. It was James and John, not Andrew, who asked Jesus for special places in the coming kingdom. Andrew seemed quietly content to be close to Jesus, serving as he could without needing the limelight. Maybe Andrew preferred not having the spotlight on him. That's a gift many of us have. And it *is* a gift.

Some of us are comfortable—and even crave—being in highly visible positions. That's good, too. We need leaders. But not all of us are called to positions of prominence. Among those of us who work behind the scenes, some may prefer it that way. Others may accept it with the grace of humility. "There is no limit to what we can accomplish if we don't care who gets the credit." (I can't remember who said this. Maybe that's the way he or she would want it.) This philosophy was apparently at the heart of Andrew's ministry.

John's Gospel is the only Gospel that mentions the story of Andrew finding Jesus and then introducing his brother Simon Peter to him. In Matthew and Mark, Jesus apparently encounters the fishermen, Andrew and Peter, at the same time. Luke's Gospel doesn't even mention Andrew by name, citing Peter as the owner of the boat. Andrew's devotion is still apparent.

Jesus had many followers, but chose twelve to be apostles. Of those twelve, it seems that Peter, James, and John were the inner core. These three were present at especially significant times, such as witnessing the Transfiguration. The only time Andrew's name is included with this inner core is when they approached Jesus to ask when the destruction of the Temple would take place. Andrew was there to receive the warning that they would be arrested, beaten, and stand before rulers

for the sake of the Gospel (Mark 13:3–4, 9). It was a dubious privilege. But Andrew's faith wasn't based on perks. Evidently he believed—like his brother Peter did—that Jesus alone had the words to eternal life. With that hope as a backdrop, circumstances in the here and now gain perspective.

Useful Service

Before feeding the five thousand, Jesus put Philip on the spot by asking him where they could buy enough food to feed all those people. Andrew chimed in with a constructive, albeit insufficient, solution. He directed their attention to the boy with a few loaves of bread and a couple of fish. Andrew humbly acknowledged the limitations of what he could offer, but offered it nonetheless. Jesus accepted and worked with Andrew's suggestion, so that it was not only sufficient, but more than enough (John 6:5–13).

The only other time Andrew is mentioned was when he again helped Philip. When some Greeks went to Philip and asked to see Jesus, Philip went to Andrew, and together they went to Jesus (John 12:20–22). Perhaps Philip saw something in Andrew that made him approachable. It may even have been the fact that Andrew stayed in the background.

It may be no accident that we hear more about Andrew in John than in the other Gospels. The author of John's Gospel has traditionally been identified with one of the inner core, the beloved disciple, one close to Jesus's heart. It makes sense that someone closest to Jesus would value Andrew's humble service behind the scenes.

Like Andrew, we may never get much recognition for faithfully answering God's call. That's good news. Jesus warned the Pharisees—who did their good deeds for show—that recognition was the only reward of such deeds. Andrew apparently had his heart set on a deeper reward. May our hope be strengthened toward that same vision.

Questions for Reflection and Discussion

1. Andrew seemed content to serve in a supporting role. When have you felt content to be in the background? Were you able to see the importance of your role at the time? How about now, as you look back?

2. Have you ever felt that you didn't get the recognition you deserved? What helped you work through your feelings?

3. Where do you think Andrew's self-esteem came from?

4. Faced with the challenge of feeding a hungry multitude, Andrew offered something positive, even though his suggestion clearly seemed inadequate. Why is doing what you can with what you have better than holding back because of fear that it's not good enough?

5. When some Greeks—presumably foreigners—asked Philip to see Jesus, Philip took them to Andrew. What do you think made Andrew approachable?

CHAPTER NINETEEN

Nathanael
Outspoken Skeptic, but Sincere Believer

Philip found Nathanael and said to him, "We have found him about whom Moses in the law and also the prophets wrote, Jesus son of Joseph from Nazareth." Nathanael said to him, "Can anything good come out of Nazareth?" Philip said to him, "Come and see." When Jesus saw Nathanael coming toward him, he said of him, "Here is truly an Israelite in whom there is no deceit!" Nathanael asked him, "Where did you come to know me?" Jesus answered, "I saw you under the fig tree before Philip called you." Nathanael replied, "Rabbi, you are the Son of God! You are the King of Israel!" Jesus answered, "Do you believe because I told you that I saw you under the fig tree? You will see greater things than these." And he said to him, "Very truly, I tell you, you will see heaven opened and the angels of God ascending and descending upon the Son of Man." (John 1:45–51)

The Skeptic

I wonder what Nathanael was thinking when he was under that fig tree. Maybe he was discouraged and thinking about giving up his faith, or just giving up period, because life was so hard. Maybe he was at a crossroads, wondering what direction the next chapter in his life should take. Maybe he just lost a job or a loved one, and was pouring out anger at God. Maybe he was just praying to know God better. We'll never know. That's the point. Whatever Nathanael was thinking was between him and Jesus. Nathanael was alone with his thoughts, in the presence of no one but God, and yet Jesus saw him, knew him, and called him to follow.

Nathanael was a devout Jew, sincere in his belief and desire for the Messiah. When he asked, "Can anything good come out of Nazareth?" Nathanael was relying on his understanding of Scripture, foretelling the Messiah's birth in Bethlehem. Nathanael had no way of knowing that Jesus had been born in Bethlehem, and so fulfilled the prophecy. But Nathanael's understanding of Scripture was limited. When Isaiah spoke about the coming Messiah, he referred to the honor that would come to the land of Galilee [where Nazareth is located] (see Isaiah 9:1). Although Nathanael was sincere in his skepticism about Jesus, he was in error because his own understanding of Scripture was limited.

Jesus was attracted by Nathanael's sincerity, not deterred by his honest doubt. Jesus wasn't looking to surround himself with yes-men. Whatever Nathanael was thinking under that fig tree, it didn't stop Jesus. Jesus valued Nathanael's ability to speak what was on his mind, instead of agreeing with Philip to avoid making waves. Nathanael's spirit didn't need changing, just his mistaken understanding of God's plan. This is good news for us as followers of Jesus.

Jesus called Nathanael a true Israelite with nothing false about him. The nation of Israel bears the name of its ancestor. Israel is the name God gave to Jacob. Jacob connived his way through life until a turning point, when he wrestled with God's angel and, though wounded, would not let go until he received a blessing. That is when God changed his name from Jacob to "Israel," which loosely translated means, "He struggles with God" (see Genesis 32:24–31).

Nathanael is a "true" Israelite. He struggled with God, and it was not held against him. Instead, he, like Jacob, was rewarded by seeing God face-to-face. And just as Jacob—now Israel—became the patriarch of a great nation, so Nathanael was called and chosen to be one of the twelve patriarchs of the new covenant.

In Good Company

This is great news for us as followers of Jesus. It means our struggles and doubts, no matter how secret, are not hidden from God; no matter

how deep, they do not ruin our chances of being called, blessed, and used by God. Honest doubt brings us close to God because Jesus is the Truth.

The apostle Thomas and his doubt are well known; even seeing wasn't believing for Thomas. He frankly admitted he would not believe Jesus had risen unless he not only saw the scars, but touched them as well. Jesus addressed this doubt (see John 20:24–29). So if we are telling the truth, whether it's about our doubt or even our anger at God, that's OK. Jesus will meet us there, and bring us through.

If our understanding of Scripture is limited, we are in good company. The Risen Christ appeared to his confused and saddened followers on the road to Emmaus. Jesus took the time to explain to them the connection between what had been written about the Messiah in the Hebrew Scripture and how it related to him. Even though they hadn't recognized him until after he broke bread with them, his explanation of the Scriptures had been "like a fire burning" in them (see Luke 24:13–35).

Jesus is the Light. He will enlighten our understanding and teach our hearts all we need to know. If we are at a crossroads and don't know which way to turn, Jesus will meet us there. Jesus said, "I am the way" (John 14:6). The Way is a living person.

I'm reminded here of a story about a little girl who went for a walk with her grandfather.

"Do you know where you are?" he asked her.

"No," she answered.

"Do you know how to get home from here?"

"No," she said again.

Her grandfather smiled and gently teased her. "It sounds to me like you're lost," he said.

She smiled back. "I'm not lost, Grandpa. I'm with you!"

Sometimes we might not know specifically where we are headed. If we stay close to the Lord, we will get to where he wants us to be. He will show us the path he has in mind for us. Like Nathanael, all we need to do is follow.

Questions for Reflection and Discussion

1. Nathanael doubted that anything good could come from Nazareth. When have you seen something good come from an unlikely source? How can being open-minded increase your awareness of God's gifts?

2. Nathanael wasn't shy about admitting his doubts concerning Jesus to his friend Philip. In which circumstances are you most comfortable sharing your own doubts? In which circumstances are you uncomfortable sharing your doubts? What makes the difference?

3. In spite of his skepticism, Nathanael was willing to investigate further, and went with Philip to meet Jesus. Is there some aspect of your life that warrants further investigation at this time? If so, what steps can you take to get more information?

4. When have you struggled with God? What happened?

CHAPTER TWENTY

Samaritan Woman
Outcast Reconciled by Truth

So he came to a Samaritan city called Sychar, near the plot of ground that Jacob had given to his son Joseph. Jacob's well was there, and Jesus, tired out by his journey, was sitting by the well. It was about noon.

A Samaritan woman came to draw water, and Jesus said to her, "Give me a drink." (His disciples had gone to the city to buy food.) The Samaritan woman said to him, "How is it that you, a Jew, ask a drink of me, a woman of Samaria?" (Jews do not share things in common with Samaritans.) Jesus answered her, "If you knew the gift of God, and who it is that is saying to you, 'Give me a drink,' you would have asked him, and he would have given you living water." The woman said to him, "Sir, you have no bucket, and the well is deep. Where do you get that living water? Are you greater than our ancestor Jacob, who gave us the well, and with his sons and his flocks drank from it?" Jesus said to her, "Everyone who drinks of this water will be thirsty again, but those who drink of the water that I will give them will never be thirsty. The water that I will give will become in them a spring of water gushing up to eternal life." The woman said to him, "Sir, give me this water, so that I may never be thirsty or have to keep coming here to draw water."

Jesus said to her, "Go, call your husband, and come back." The woman answered him, "I have no husband." Jesus said to her, "You are right in saying, 'I have no husband'; for you have had five husbands, and the one you have now is not

your husband. What you have said is true!" The woman said to him, "Sir, I see that you are a prophet. Our ancestors worshiped on this mountain, but you say that the place where people must worship is in Jerusalem." Jesus said to her, "Woman, believe me, the hour is coming when you will worship the Father neither on this mountain nor in Jerusalem. You worship what you do not know; we worship what we know, for salvation is from the Jews. But the hour is coming, and is now here, when the true worshipers will worship the Father in spirit and truth, for the Father seeks such as these to worship him. God is spirit, and those who worship him must worship in spirit and truth." The woman said to him, "I know that Messiah is coming" (who is called Christ). "When he comes, he will proclaim all things to us." Jesus said to her, "I am he, the one who is speaking to you."

Just then his disciples came. They were astonished that he was speaking with a woman, but no one said, "What do you want?" or, "Why are you speaking with her?" Then the woman left her water jar and went back to the city. She said to the people, "Come and see a man who told me everything I have ever done! He cannot be the Messiah, can he?" They left the city and were on their way to him. (John 4:5–30)

The Triple Threat

Jesus initiates contact with a triple threat to propriety: a Samaritan, an unescorted woman, and apparently the town tramp. She came to get water at noon to avoid the other townspeople, who would have gotten their water in the cool of the morning. He asked her for a drink, which surprised her. She was probably surprised that anybody would talk to her—especially a Jew—even if it was to ask for a favor.

As a social outcast, she must have been used to being ignored if not outright rejected.

Five husbands? She probably wasn't shy about talking to men, and apparently Jesus was no different to her, at least initially. Maybe the only way she had ever been able to get attention at all was by using her feminine wiles. When Jesus asked her to get her husband and she answered that she had no husband. I can't help wondering if she might have been flirting with Jesus.

In spite of that, it seems to me this woman thirsted for something better than the life she had. When offered life-giving water, she eagerly accepted the offer, if only to get out of coming to the well every day. I wonder if she sensed that Jesus was offering something other than easy access to well water. If that was all he offered, why did he ask her for a drink in the first place?

After Jesus saw through her deceptive response about having a husband, the woman realized that Jesus was relating to her on a much deeper plane. He touched something deep inside her, something I think her heart craved. Nevertheless, it must have threatened her to have someone probe so close to her heart. She turned the conversation to theological debate about sects and places of worship. Jesus did not take sides on the issue but spoke about true worship for all people through God's Spirit.

The woman may have been mistaken about the practicalities of religion. Nevertheless, she had faith and hope in the Messiah. Unlike many self-righteous religious and community leaders, she did not miss him when he revealed himself to her. She trusted the evidence of her own experience. Jesus had approached her without looking down on her. He was not thrown off track by her manipulations. He spoke with insight and genuine concern for who she really was, apart from her affectations and the community's assessment of her. He cut to the heart of her being, and her heart responded.

The power of Jesus's love is bigger than our images of our own self-worth. It is bigger than our fears and our attempts to protect ourselves from rejection. This woman knew the truth when she heard it and the news was too good to keep to herself. She had something important to share and she hurried to the townspeople she previously avoided.

After her encounter with Jesus, she didn't worry about rejection, gossip, or scornful looks. The woman had the courage to risk social rejection because—maybe for the first time in her life—she felt she had something genuinely worthwhile to offer. Her own conviction convinced others. The townspeople followed her. She didn't have to try to be something she was not. Part of the miracle was that Jesus met her in her isolation and shame. She didn't have to hide it anymore. What she had been wasn't as important as what she had the opportunity to become—his ambassador. She acted on that and people responded.

The Truth Sets Us Free

It is so easy to think we have to cover up our shortcomings in order to be effective or set a good example. Maybe the best example we can set is to be honest about our weaknesses and struggles. In that way, we can share what God is doing in us and for us. Jesus said that if we obeyed him we would know the truth and that it would set us free (John 8:31–32). He also said, "I am...the truth" (John 14:6). The Truth is Christ. As we come to know Christ and experience unconditional love, we will enjoy the freedom of being authentic without fear of rejection. Like the Samaritan woman, we will lose the need to protect ourselves from shame by isolating or clinging to false fronts and self-righteousness.

That level of sincerity may be the key to the effectiveness of some self-help groups, such as the Twelve Step programs. People genuinely expose their own vulnerability in a safe atmosphere of unconditional acceptance. Thus encouraged, they can begin to face and deal with

problems rather than deny them. Trust develops as they mutually seek and share solutions. These are powerful antidotes to isolation.

Nevertheless, there's a time and a place for sharing. We don't have to broadcast our secrets or land ourselves on the cover of a gossip magazine. But when guided by the Holy Spirit, we can prudently risk sharing our faults in order to ask for help for ourselves, and when it might help others. Our sincerity can encourage others to acknowledge their own weaknesses. Trusting God to meet us exactly where we are and bring us forward is truly good news worth sharing.

Questions for Reflection and Discussion

1. When the Samaritan woman first encountered Jesus, her interest in the water he offered seemed to be based on practical self-interest. What are some self-serving ways that people approach God today?

2. When Jesus brought the interaction closer to her heart, the woman retreated to theological debate. How can dwelling on religious dogmas obscure authentic spiritual development?

3. The woman's awareness of who Jesus was developed in stages. How has your own awareness of who Jesus is deepened over time?

4. After her encounter with Jesus, the woman reached out to others. Why is genuine sharing from the heart so important in spreading the good news?

CHAPTER TWENTY-ONE

Man at Pool
Chronic Invalid Who Was Healed

Now in Jerusalem by the Sheep Gate there is a pool, called in Hebrew Beth-zatha, which has five porticoes. In these lay many invalids—blind, lame, and paralyzed. One man was there who had been ill for thirty-eight years. When Jesus saw him lying there and knew that he had been there a long time, he said to him, "Do you want to be made well?" The sick man answered him, "Sir, I have no one to put me into the pool when the water is stirred up; and while I am making my way, someone else steps down ahead of me." Jesus said to him, "Stand up, take your mat and walk." At once the man was made well, and he took up his mat and began to walk.

Now that day was a sabbath. So the Jews said to the man who had been cured, "It is the sabbath; it is not lawful for you to carry your mat." But he answered them, "The man who made me well said to me, 'Take up your mat and walk.'" They asked him, "Who is the man who said to you, 'Take it up and walk'?" Now the man who had been healed did not know who it was, for Jesus had disappeared in the crowd that was there. Later Jesus found him in the temple and said to him, "See, you have been made well! Do not sin any more, so that nothing worse happens to you." The man went away and told the Jews that it was Jesus who had made him well. Therefore the Jews started persecuting Jesus, because he was doing such things on the sabbath. But Jesus answered them, "My Father is still working, and I also am working." (John 5:2–17)

Status Quo or Healed?

We don't even know this man's name. Nevertheless, he is called. Whether or not he had been sick since birth, thirty-eight years is a long time to live with a disability.

"Do you want to be made well?" What a strange question to ask an invalid. Why wouldn't anybody want to get well? Wouldn't "Of course I do!" be anybody's answer? Maybe not. It is human nature to become accustomed to things as they are.

Somehow, the man had survived for thirty-eight years with the status quo. Yes, he was in the place where healing miracles occasionally happened. But when asked if he wanted to get well, the man didn't say, "Of course!" He offered a reason (or excuse?) as to why he hadn't been healed already. He told Jesus that when the pool was stirred up there was nobody to help him. Someone else always got in first and was healed.

If the man had no one to help him into the pool, chances are he had no one to bring him to the pool and back home every day. Maybe he had no home. Maybe he just lived on his mat on the porch for thirty-eight years, eating whatever providence sent his way, living off the alms of passersby.

It was not the most desirable way of life, but a way of life nonetheless. He knew what to expect. Healing, wonderful as it might be, meant a brand new set of circumstances and an onslaught of new challenges. If he was no longer sick, he would no longer receive alms. How would he earn a living? Leaving the familiar, uncomfortable as it might be, can be intimidating.

Nevertheless, something in the man's response signaled to Jesus that he was open for healing. When Jesus instructed the man to get up, pick up his mat, and walk, the man immediately obeyed. Jesus short-circuited the invalid's expectations and he responded. If the man debated with himself about how healing could happen outside

the pool, his leap of faith could have been a faltering crawl that led nowhere. Fortunately, he seized the opportunity when it came and did not debate with Jesus or with himself. He gave it a try and it worked.

The man also picked up his mat as he was told. What could be more psychologically sound than for Jesus to instruct the man to pick up his mat? He no longer needed to permanently camp out by the pool. Now that healing had occurred, he needed to pull up stakes and move on. What if he had left his mat there because it was against the Jewish law to carry his mat on a Sabbath? The security of his old familiar spot might have called him back to his former lifestyle. This might have paved the way for doubt that his newfound healing would last. But he obeyed Jesus.

Resistance to Further Healing

When religious authorities questioned the man, he tried to pass the buck, but was unable to identify Jesus at the time. The man had availed himself of Jesus's healing power without knowing Jesus's name. His ignorance did not keep him from being a witness to Jesus. It did prevent the authorities from persecuting Jesus initially.

When Jesus next encountered him, the man was in the Temple, maybe thanking God for his healing. Jesus approached the man and advised him to stop sinning or "something worse" might happen to him. I wonder what sins kept the man on precarious ground. Jesus surrendered the protection of anonymity to warn the man of a fate worse than physical disability. When God heals, he wants more for us than we want for ourselves. Jesus wanted this man to be healed of whatever weakness blocked him from a fuller experience of God's love. Jesus called him to an inner healing.

However, once armed with the knowledge of Jesus's identity, the man turned Jesus in to the Jewish authorities. Although willing to be healed physically, he did not seem willing or ready to heal on a deeper emotional level. Maybe giving up the sin and error that blocked him

from further recovery was a price he was unwilling to pay. Jesus called him to further growth. The man chose to cling to the status quo of religious tradition as interpreted by the Jewish authorities. Gratitude for the physical healing was not enough. Perhaps he loved the security of the established order too much to move forward in his development.

Recovery Is a Process

Jesus didn't undo the man's physical healing after he turned Jesus in. The man sentenced himself to stunted growth. He could not progress beyond the level of healing he was willing to accept and act on. Recovery sometimes happens in stages. This is illustrated in another of Jesus's miracles.

Jesus once placed his hands on a blind man whose vision was restored, but not all at once. At first the man told Jesus that he could see people, but they looked walking trees. Jesus placed his hands on the man's eyes a second time and then he was able to see clearly (Mark 8:22–25).

Recovery is a process. While there are circumstances beyond our control, there are things we can do to cooperate with our own recovery. On a physical level, we can follow medical advice. We can rest, eat properly, take appropriate medications, and get a reasonable amount of exercise. On an emotional and spiritual level there are also things we can do to cooperate with or resist healthy growth. We can determine whether or not to indulge in negative thoughts and behavior. We can decide to spend our free time on uplifting and nurturing pursuits or else choose to put ourselves in risky environments. When necessary, we can seek help in overcoming resistance to healthy choices.

Maybe, with God's help, the man healed at Beth-zatha eventually grew enough to let go of whatever sin was holding him back. Whether he did or didn't, we can review our own choices.

Questions for Reflection and Discussion

1. Have you ever felt stuck with no human power seemingly able to help you move forward? What was the outcome?

2. What does it take for someone to answer when Christ invites him or her to get up, leave his or her resting place, and move forward?

3. When have you felt prompted to take a risk that would lead to healing, such as leaving a familiar but unhealthy relationship or job situation? Did you act on that prompting? Did you second-guess? What happened?

4. Are you being called now to continued growth by moving in a new direction?

CHAPTER TWENTY-TWO

Joseph of Arimathea
Prominent Jew, Disciple of Jesus

When evening had come, and since it was the day of Preparation, that is, the day before the sabbath, Joseph of Arimathea, a respected member of the council, who was also himself waiting expectantly for the kingdom of God, went boldly to Pilate and asked for the body of Jesus. Then Pilate wondered if he were already dead; and summoning the centurion, he asked him whether he had been dead for some time. When he learned from the centurion that he was dead, he granted the body to Joseph. Then Joseph bought a linen cloth, and taking down the body, wrapped it in the linen cloth, and laid it in a tomb that had been hewn out of the rock. He then rolled a stone against the door of the tomb. (Mark 15:42–46)

After these things, Joseph of Arimathea, who was a disciple of Jesus, though a secret one because of his fear of the Jews, asked Pilate to let him take away the body of Jesus. Pilate gave him permission; so he came and removed his body. Nicodemus, who had at first come to Jesus by night, also came, bringing a mixture of myrrh and aloes, weighing about a hundred pounds. They took the body of Jesus and wrapped it with the spices in linen cloths, according to the burial custom of the Jews. Now there was a garden in the place where he was crucified, and in the garden there was a new tomb in which no one had ever been laid. And so, because it was the Jewish day of Preparation, and the tomb was nearby, they laid Jesus there. (John 19:38–42)

The Prominent Jew

Joseph initially followed Jesus in secret, because he was afraid of the Jewish authorities. But Joseph *was* a Jewish authority. He was a member of the Sanhedrin, the Jewish council. Who better than Joseph would know what the members of the council could do? He had seen what went on behind their closed doors. He knew firsthand their power to manipulate, to use pressure, and to carry out threats. The Jewish leaders were the keepers of the covenant handed down from Moses. Until Christ, there was no other way to the one true God but through the law and traditions as administered by the Jewish leadership. Being expelled from the Temple meant being cut off from all channels to worshiping God.

Joseph of Arimathea, steeped in Jewish law and tradition, was well aware of the teaching that had been handed down. Like many other sincere Jewish believers, he was hoping for the kingdom of God. Unlike other members of the council, however, Joseph recognized the truth when he heard it. He saw beyond the extensive network of laws that tradition had crystallized over the centuries.

Joseph must have sensed that Jesus's words and life embodied the heart of the law while cutting through the minutiae. Jesus had condensed the law to the essence of loving God with our whole being, and loving our neighbors as ourselves (see Matthew 22:36–40). Obeying this law of love fulfills the Ten Commandments from which all other laws derive. If we give God first place, if we treat others and ourselves with respect and concern, we will not steal, kill, bear false witness, or destroy relationships over possessions.

Joseph saw this and believed, but overcoming a mind-set instilled over a lifetime is no small task. Nor is it easy to remain on the fence, torn between two choices. Joseph witnessed the council predetermine justice and demand Jesus's execution. Filled with fear, jealousy, and close-mindedness, the council members conspired together to hand Jesus over to the Roman governor. Joseph stood at the turning point.

Mark's Gospel states that Joseph went *boldly* into Pilate's presence. This was a daring move in more ways than one. Joseph chose to speak out, knowing what this very public act on behalf of Christ would mean. It would mean the end of Joseph's participation in the council and acceptance by his peers. It could mean expulsion from the Temple and the end of familiar and traditional forms of worship for him. It might also mean persecution.

I can imagine the emotional turmoil he might have felt. But Joseph's devotion to the God of his understanding would not allow him to disregard his own conscience. An innocent man had been put to death. Joseph could not undo that. Instead, he did what he could.

When he went to see Pilate it was already late in the day. Since the Sabbath began at sundown, it was crucial for Jews to cease work before then, especially on this important Sabbath, the Passover. Pilate sent for the army officer to confirm Jesus's death. More delay. Joseph, still wishing to be an observant Jew, might have felt increasingly anxious, torn between his desire to give Jesus a decent burial yet not violate Sabbath law. Nevertheless, he remained steadfast until he accomplished what his heart and conscience told him was the right thing to do.

Perfect Timing

Perhaps Joseph could have acted on his conversion sooner if he had more courage and less regard for the opinions of the establishment. I wonder if it was fear or hope in working within the system that prevented Joseph from acting sooner. But I believe God took his delay in going public into consideration. The timing was perfect for Joseph to accomplish the crucial task of claiming Jesus's body and providing for its burial.

Had Joseph *not* been a member of the council, he would not have had sufficient clout to do what he did. Going into the presence of Pilate and requesting Jesus's body was not something any of Christ's

other followers could have done. Joseph held a position of authority and prestige. If he had taken a stand sooner, he might not have been in that position. Joseph was called to use his status to serve God's purpose. When the time was right, he risked it all to answer the call.

Joseph of Arimathea ultimately followed his conscience in opposition to making the politically expedient choice. He gave Jesus a decent burial. Thanks to his action, Mary Magdalene and others were able to see where Jesus's body was placed. It seems to me that all this was part of God's plan. Joseph's action ensured that Jesus would be buried in a place where his followers would be able to see the empty tomb three days later.

If Joseph had not requested the body, who knows what would have happened to it? Where were the bodies of other executed prisoners buried? If they were in an unknown or a mass grave, what obstacles might there have been to confirming that Jesus rose again? We know there was an empty tomb thanks to Joseph of Arimathea's bold action.

There comes a time when we need to act. Faith without works is dead (see James 2:26). If we don't act on what we believe, maybe we don't really believe it. If we believe God is in control, we may need to stop trying to engineer or force outcomes. If we believe that loving others is more important than status or success, we may need to reconsider our priorities and where we invest our time and energy.

But aligning our actions with our beliefs is easier said than done. Some of us take longer than others to act on our convictions. A number of factors can contribute to delays. We don't have to second-guess why Joseph didn't act sooner. Nor do we have to second-guess ourselves when we have failed to act promptly. We all have regrets. Joseph hesitated before finally taking action.

God can work though followers like him and like us, who sometimes hesitate. I believe he takes this into account and can use it to fulfill his plan. The parable of the workers in the vineyard is finally

making more sense to me. Those who started working late in the day got paid as much as those who started working in the morning (see Matthew 20:1–16). God extends his patience and generosity to us all. It's never too late to let go of past failures. We can always make a choice to do the right thing in the present moment. When we do, God can bring it to good purpose.

Questions for Reflection and Discussion

1. After he had followed Jesus in secret for some time, what do you suppose enabled Joseph to boldly approach Pilate and ask for Jesus's body?
2. When is it appropriate to take a stand against those in authority? What is involved?
3. Think of a time when you, or someone you know, were in a position to offer assistance to another. How did past experience or present status impact the ability to serve in that particular situation? What does this say about God acting "behind the scenes"?
4. Why is it important not to judge others who have delayed in making changes for the better in their lives?

CHAPTER TWENTY-THREE

Philip (Deacon)
Witness of the Holy Spirit

Then an angel of the Lord said to Philip, "Get up and go towards the south to the road that goes down from Jerusalem to Gaza." (This is a wilderness road.) So he got up and went. Now there was an Ethiopian eunuch, a court official of the Candace, queen of the Ethiopians, in charge of her entire treasury. He had come to Jerusalem to worship and was returning home; seated in his chariot, he was reading the prophet Isaiah. Then the Spirit said to Philip, "Go over to this chariot and join it." So Philip ran up to it and heard him reading the prophet Isaiah. He asked, "Do you understand what you are reading?" He replied, "How can I, unless someone guides me?" And he invited Philip to get in and sit beside him. Now the passage of the scripture that he was reading was this:
"Like a sheep he was led to the slaughter,
    and like a lamb silent before its shearer,
        so he does not open his mouth.
In his humiliation justice was denied him.
    Who can describe his generation?
        For his life is taken away from the earth."
The eunuch asked Philip, "About whom, may I ask you, does the prophet say this, about himself or about someone else?" Then Philip began to speak, and starting with this scripture, he proclaimed to him the good news about Jesus. As they were going along the road, they came to some water; and the eunuch said, "Look, here is water! What is to prevent

me from being baptized?" He commanded the chariot to stop, and both of them, Philip and the eunuch, went down into the water, and Philip baptized him. When they came up out of the water, the Spirit of the Lord snatched Philip away; the eunuch saw him no more, and went on his way rejoicing. But Philip found himself at Azotus, and as he was passing through the region, he proclaimed the good news to all the towns until he came to Caesarea. (Acts 8:26–40)

The Philip mentioned in this story is not the same Philip who was one of the twelve apostles. According to the Acts of the Apostles, this Philip was one of the seven deacons originally appointed by the apostles to help distribute funds to the community of believers. This would enable the apostles to give their full time to prayer and preaching. Philip and the other six deacons were chosen because they were "full of the Spirit and of wisdom" (see Acts 6:2–6).

The Holy Spirit did not confine using Philip's wisdom to distributing funds. The Spirit also did not confine Philip to sharing his wisdom with Jewish believers. Acts records Philip preaching, baptizing, and performing miracles among Samaritans, people looked down upon by Jews (see Acts 8:5–13). Philip was among the first to preach beyond the Jewish community. Following the promptings of the Holy Spirit, Philip was moved to share the good news regardless of the background of his audience. The passage that begins this chapter describes how Philip similarly spread the good news to another foreigner, the Ethiopian official.

The Holy Spirit led Philip to go on the road from Jerusalem to Gaza. Scripture doesn't say that Philip knew why. Maybe he thought his goal was to get to Gaza. But he felt nudged to be on that road at that time, and he obeyed. Once he acted on that initial prompting, Philip was given further instructions to stay close to a certain carriage.

He obeyed again and heard the Ethiopian official reading from Isaiah. Philip was not put off by the official's rank; or the fact that the official was African; or the fact that he was a eunuch. Philip focused on the inner prompting of the Holy Spirit.

He asked the official if he understood what he was reading. By responding to the official's question, Philip met him where he was. Starting with his question about a particular passage of Scripture, Philip then shared the good news about Jesus with his listener.

We aren't told much about Philip's background. His name suggests he was Greek-speaking, and therefore more open to a wider circle of ministry than the Jews in Jerusalem. Although a deacon in charge of finances, he was gifted with the ability to preach and work miracles. The beauty of his preaching can be seen in his willingness to meet his audience where he was and then lead him further into the truth.

When sharing our faith, it is tempting to start with what we know and funnel it out to others. This obscures any common ground we share with our audience. It might also invite them to tune us out, since people generally don't like being talked down to.

The good news is a message of love. It seems to me that demonstrating love for our listeners begins with respecting them by approaching them as equally beloved children of God. Philip did this by starting with the Ethiopian official's point of view. The generosity and tolerance it takes to be centered on others is part of the wisdom received from the Holy Spirit. Philip definitely was not running the show. He did not take charge, but was sensitive to both internal and external cues. Rather than imposing his belief, Philip gently persuaded the Ethiopian official to a more complete understanding of God's message.

Philip was empathetic yet forthright. His reliance on the Holy Spirit gave him the courage to act on his convictions, albeit with sensitivity. He baptized the Ethiopian official who went on his way full of

joy. Philip also went on his way, trusting the Holy Spirit to continue to guide them both.

Going With the Flow

Following the Spirit's nudge, Philip "found himself" in Azotus, no doubt sharing the good news wherever the Spirit moved him. This going with the flow apparently was effective without leading to insta-bility. The Spirit eventually led Philip to Caesarea. We catch up with Philip much later in Acts, still residing there, with his four unmarried daughters who also proclaimed God's word. Philip, besides whatever else he did in the interim, established a home and was able to provide for Paul and his companions when they arrived in Caesarea, presum-ably some years later (Acts 21:8–9).

Structure is a necessary part of life. As a deacon, Philip had the responsibility of distributing funds to needy believers. I am sure orga-nized planning was necessary in performing this duty. Yet Philip also seemed able to go with the flow. There are times that require flexibility. This can be challenging for some people, but letting go of control doesn't mean surrendering to chaos. Flying by the seat of our pants isn't haphazard if we are relying on the Holy Spirit for guidance. Some of us are more comfortable with detailed marching orders in advance. Some of us go with the flow more easily, without relying on clearly defined itineraries. There is room for both in God's kingdom.

Questions for Reflection and Discussion

1. What do you suppose enabled Philip to hear the angel's instruc-tions? What qualities are involved in being open to the Holy Spirit's promptings?

2. Think of a time when someone tried to share a differing point of view with you. Whether or not you ultimately agreed with them, how easy or difficult was it for you to relate to what they were sharing? What made it easy or difficult?

3. In sharing the good news with others, why can it be more effective to find some common ground as a starting point?

4. What are the biggest obstacles to initiating communication by starting from another person's point of view? Name some ways to overcome these challenges.

5. How challenging is it for you to go with the flow when your plans are interrupted? What are some ways to adjust to unexpected changes?

CHAPTER TWENTY-FOUR

Ananias
Doubter, but Obedient Servant

Meanwhile Saul, still breathing threats and murder against the disciples of the Lord, went to the high priest and asked him for letters to the synagogues at Damascus, so that if he found any who belonged to the Way, men or women, he might bring them bound to Jerusalem. Now as he was going along and approaching Damascus, suddenly a light from heaven flashed around him. He fell to the ground and heard a voice saying to him, "Saul, Saul, why do you persecute me?" He asked, "Who are you, Lord?" The reply came, "I am Jesus, whom you are persecuting. But get up and enter the city, and you will be told what you are to do." The men who were traveling with him stood speechless because they heard the voice but saw no one. Saul got up from the ground, and though his eyes were open, he could see nothing; so they led him by the hand and brought him into Damascus. For three days he was without sight, and neither ate nor drank.

Now there was a disciple in Damascus named Ananias. The Lord said to him in a vision, "Ananias." He answered, "Here I am, Lord." The Lord said to him, "Get up and go to the street called Straight, and at the house of Judas look for a man of Tarsus named Saul. At this moment he is praying, and he has seen in a vision a man named Ananias come in and lay his hands on him so that he might regain his sight." But Ananias answered, "Lord, I have heard from many about this man, how much evil he has done to your saints in Jerusalem; and here he has authority from the chief priests to

bind all who invoke your name." But the Lord said to him, "Go, for he is an instrument whom I have chosen to bring my name before Gentiles and kings and before the people of Israel; I myself will show him how much he must suffer for the sake of my name." So Ananias went and entered the house. He laid his hands on Saul and said, "Brother Saul, the Lord Jesus, who appeared to you on your way here, has sent me so that you may regain your sight and be filled with the Holy Spirit." And immediately something like scales fell from his eyes, and his sight was restored. Then he got up and was baptized, and after taking some food, he regained his strength. (Acts 9:1–19)

"Here I Am, Lord"

When Jesus called him by name, Ananias knew who was calling. He responded immediately. "Here I am, Lord." So far, so good. Then the Lord asked Ananias to walk into the lion's den. It is easy to imagine the struggle behind Ananias's initial reaction: "Wait a minute, Lord. You want me to go *where*? And see *whom*? This Saul has done terrible things to your followers. His blindness is the only thing keeping us safe. Now you want me to *heal* him? Are you sure this is a good idea?"

There was good reason for Ananias to feel threatened. He had no proof that Saul's blindness had changed his attitude. Even if being knocked down, questioned by God, and struck blind had softened Saul's heart, there was no guarantee that his companions were prepared to be open-minded. Saul's host and quite possibly the entire neighborhood were probably antagonistic toward Christ's followers.

Even if Ananias trusted God for his personal safety, I can understand questioning the wisdom of putting Saul—a threat to other Christians—back in commission. At least while incapacitated, Saul could do no harm. Saul's blindness might have seemed like a miracle

wrought to spare the believers in Damascus. I wouldn't blame Ananias if he had trouble seeing how God's plan involved healing Saul.

But Jesus's plan wasn't to protect believers from all possible harm. He didn't protect his own body from harm while on earth. He would treat his followers, the body of Christ, the same way. Christ's purpose was and is to spread the good news so that every open heart can receive the gift of eternal life. By restoring Saul's sight, God turned him from an instrument of persecution into an instrument of spreading the good news.

Ananias is not the first person to resist God's marching orders. When God told Moses he was sending him to the pharaoh to rescue the Hebrew slaves, Moses responded with numerous objections. One by one, God addressed each of Moses's concerns by reassuring him with further information about his plan (Exodus 3:7—4:17).

In a similar way, the Lord revealed more about his purpose and plan to Ananias. He explained that he had chosen Saul to be his ambassador not only to Israelites, but to Gentiles, as well. God also assured Ananias that Saul would not be exempt from further suffering as he spread the good news for the sake of his name. God does not play favorites.

It took three days for Ananias to finally do what he was called to do. I can relate to his hesitancy, but I also suspect God was using that time. As Ananias was undergoing his own conversion experience, Saul was learning to see with the eyes of faith. When the time was right for both of them, Ananias stepped out in faithful obedience.

Answering the Call

When he entered the house, Ananias greeted him as "Brother Saul." What a change of heart! Ananias placed his hands on Saul and restored his sight. Saul was then filled with the Holy Spirit. Why didn't God bestow the Holy Spirit directly on Saul when he appeared to him on the road? That's how the apostles received the Holy Spirit

(John 20:21–23; Acts 2:1–4). Why did God choose to work through Ananias?

Among other reasons, I suspect that both Saul and Ananias needed to go through the experience. Just as Saul learned to be open to God's Spirit working through followers of the Way, Ananias learned to be open to the Holy Spirit working through the likes of a Pharisee. We all need to learn to keep open to the Spirit in us that is always doing something new.

Ananias knew God was calling him but still felt fear and questioned the wisdom of God's plan. He faced his reluctance honestly and brought it to God. Ananias took the time he needed to grow in grace and overcome his resistance. He ultimately obeyed.

We can take heart from Ananias. It is OK to face our doubts and fears and reason them out with God or with trusted spiritual guide. God will meet us at our roadblocks and either remove them or enable us to overcome them. God will not ask more of us than we are able to provide. After all, God called Ananias to heal Saul, a daunting enough challenge. God reserved for himself the unsavory task of telling Saul all the suffering that was in store for him.

The Lord may be inviting us to reach out to someone today. Maybe it's someone we might not think needs our help, or that we even find threatening. It might be the perfectly dressed soccer mom whose kids always sit still at church while ours fidget and squirm. It might be the sullen teen with the dark eye makeup and the darker scowl that our daughter befriended. Maybe it's the colleague at work that is a little too charming or the pastor who seems so full of wisdom we suspect he has all the answers to life.

Who might need our understanding and help today? It might be the one we least expect.

Questions for Reflection and Discussion

1. Like Ananias, have you ever wrestled with something you felt God was prompting you to do? What happened?

2. Where do you find encouragement when it isn't easy to see God's purpose?

3. It took three days for Ananias to approach Saul and lay hands on him. How do you think God may have been working in this delay? What does this say to you when plans don't unfold according to your timetable?

4. How can you extend healthy tolerance to others without compromising your own values?

5. What can help you overcome discomfort when God invites you to stretch beyond your comfort zone?

CHAPTER TWENTY-FIVE

Tabitha
The Homebody Who Ministered

Now in Joppa there was a disciple whose name was Tabitha, which in Greek is Dorcas. She was devoted to good works and acts of charity. At that time she became ill and died. When they had washed her, they laid her in a room upstairs. Since Lydda was near Joppa, the disciples, who heard that Peter was there, sent two men to him with the request, "Please come to us without delay." So Peter got up and went with them; and when he arrived, they took him to the room upstairs. All the widows stood beside him, weeping and showing tunics and other clothing that Dorcas had made while she was with them. Peter put all of them outside, and then he knelt down and prayed. He turned to the body and said, "Tabitha, get up." Then she opened her eyes, and seeing Peter, she sat up. He gave her his hand and helped her up. Then calling the saints and widows, he showed her to be alive. This became known throughout Joppa, and many believed in the Lord. (Acts 9:36–42)

The Backbone of Christ

Tabitha never preached a sermon or wrote an epistle. There is no record that she defended the faith with winning arguments against the challenges of nonbelievers. It is quite possible that she never traveled outside her hometown. She was too busy helping others. Tabitha was called to preach through her service and was faithful to her mission. Her life made a difference. Her qualification was not spiritual insight, but the fact that she was a believer and put that belief into action.

If people like St. Thomas Aquinas are the brains of the body of Christ, and people like St. Francis are the heart, the strong, silent type of believers, like Tabitha, are the backbone. Many who work for social justice find themselves in prominent positions of leadership. Many more remain nameless, quietly doing the loving thing. They do what they can, using their abilities—whatever they may be—to serve others.

Tabitha grew where she was planted. She apparently had the domestic skills common to women in that culture. She used her sewing ability to make clothes for the needy. A simple enough task, but it made a huge impact on those within her circle. Distressed when she died, the people in her community sent for Peter and asked him to intercede.

Jesus told his disciples that those who wanted to be first needed to be last and to serve others (see Mark 9:35). Tabitha lived this teaching. It seems counterintuitive to put the well-being of others ahead of ourselves. Those who focus on a "me first" attitude are probably motivated by fear of not having enough. Like Tabitha, those who trust God to meet their needs—not necessarily their wants—have those needs met. They are able to give to others with the same generosity they feel in receiving the gifts God has given them.

But even a giver like Tabitha also needed nurturing. Being a hard worker and willing servant does not exempt people from having needs. Tabitha's case was dramatic. She was lifeless. Peter made a special trip to her bedside. If she had been conscious, I imagine her squirming at the thought of troubling anybody—let alone Peter, the head of the entire Christian community.

Tabitha's name in Greek means "deer." I picture her quiet and deer-like, anxious to keep out of the way. Maybe if she had been conscious and protested, Peter never would have been summoned at all. When she was beyond helping herself, she received ministry, and rightly so.

How appropriate. This humble servant in the body of Christ was herself served by Peter, its head. What an example for us.

Humility in Service
It is easy for some of us to become so concerned with others that we jeopardize our physical and emotional health. We need to take appropriate care of ourselves in order to be able to give to others. Being self-giving to a fault can be as harmful as being self-centered. There is a danger of losing humility.

We all need help at times. It is possible to distort self-sacrifice into a kind of reverse pride. It is a subtle form of false pride to think we can always be on the giving end. That kind of power belongs to God alone. Knowing our limitations and accepting help is an act of healthy humility. It also gives others the opportunity to be blessed by giving of themselves.

Even Jesus allowed himself to be nurtured. When he was anointed with expensive perfume, his disciples objected because the money could have been used to help the poor. Jesus responded by defending the woman who anointed him, affirming that she had done something good. Jesus also pointed out that there would always be poor people (see Matthew 26:6–12).

I believe that Jesus was acting in love for the woman who anointed him. By accepting her gift, he allowed her to experience the dignity and joy of serving another. Nevertheless, I doubt that Jesus was promoting self-indulgence above helping the poor. I understand this passage to mean—at least in part—that poverty will never be eliminated and that along with doing what we can to help others, we need to guard against grandiosity. Thinking we are up to the task of endlessly giving without taking time for self-renewal paves the way for self-righteous pride and burnout.

Ultimately, when Tabitha was helped by Peter, she was given back to the community. After receiving assistance herself, she was then able

to serve once more. When our well is dry, we have nothing to give to anyone. When our well is full and we hoard our blessings, we deprive ourselves of the gifts of sharing and we deprive others of needed help. Balance is the key.

Tabitha, humble servant of the poor, is known because the writer of Acts included her story when recording Peter's experiences. His visit to Tabitha's deathbed was one of Peter's "acts." The only reason Scripture mentions Tabitha is because she received healing. Like her, countless others live lives of quiet service without recognition. That doesn't render their service any less valuable.

Those who serve in unspectacular ways—looking after a child or relative, serving up meals at a soup kitchen, listening to a lonely voice on the phone—are indeed the greatest in the kingdom of heaven. As Jesus said, "By this everyone will know that you are my disciples, if you have love for one another" (John 13:35). Tabitha is a role model for us all.

Questions for Reflection and Discussion

1. Think of the "Tabithas" in your life. How do they preach the good news by their actions?

2. Tabitha apparently had an ability to sew. What skills or abilities do you have? How can they be used to further God's kingdom?

3. Why is it important to balance giving with receiving? What would that balance look like in your current life?

4. When she was not able to ask for help for herself, others asked Peter for help on Tabitha's behalf. Can you think of anyone unable to ask for help who needs you to intercede on their behalf?

5. Receiving help enabled Tabitha to go on living her life of service. How can reaching out for support from others help you serve better? How comfortable are you asking for and receiving help?

CHAPTER TWENTY-SIX

Mary, Mother of John Mark
Loving Mother Who Let Go

The very night before Herod was going to bring him out, Peter, bound with two chains, was sleeping between two soldiers, while guards in front of the door were keeping watch over the prison. Suddenly an angel of the Lord appeared and a light shone in the cell. He tapped Peter on the side and woke him, saying, "Get up quickly." And the chains fell off his wrists. The angel said to him, "Fasten your belt and put on your sandals." He did so. Then he said to him, "Wrap your cloak around you and follow me." Peter went out and followed him; he did not realize that what was happening with the angel's help was real; he thought he was seeing a vision. After they had passed the first and the second guard, they came before the iron gate leading into the city. It opened for them of its own accord, and they went outside and walked along a lane, when suddenly the angel left him. Then Peter came to himself and said, "Now I am sure that the Lord has sent his angel and rescued me from the hands of Herod and from all that the Jewish people were expecting."

As soon as he realized this, he went to the house of Mary, the mother of John whose other name was Mark, where many had gathered and were praying. When he knocked at the outer gate, a maid named Rhoda came to answer. On recognizing Peter's voice, she was so overjoyed that, instead of opening the gate, she ran in and announced that Peter was standing at the gate. They said to her, "You are out of your mind!" But she insisted that it was so. They said, "It is his angel." Meanwhile Peter continued knocking; and when

they opened the gate, they saw him and were amazed. He motioned to them with his hand to be silent, and described for them how the Lord had brought him out of the prison. And he added, "Tell this to James and to the believers." Then he left and went to another place. (Acts 12:6–17)

The Risk Taker

Scripture mentions Mary, the mother of John Mark, only once. Peter, the rock on whom Christ was building his Church, trusted her. He went straight to her house after escaping from prison. Her home was a meeting place for the early Christians, for whom it was not safe to practice out in the open. It was even riskier to be known as a leader. After all, Peter had been imprisoned. Stephen had been martyred. Believers, especially leaders, were being persecuted. Yet Mary risked opening her home so that other believers could gather and pray.

Mary must have been well-to-do. She owned a house big enough to be a gathering space for a number of people. She also had at least one servant, Rhoda. Sometimes wealth can be an obstacle to faith. When we have resources, it is easy to trust them and forget that our well-being and our resources are gifts from God, to be used for his purposes and to help others. The rich young man who loved Jesus but could not part with his riches missed this point and went away saddened (see Matthew 19:16–22).

In contrast, Mary's cousin Barnabas sold the field he owned and turned the money over to the apostles (see Acts 4:36–37). Barnabas then traveled extensively, preaching the good news. Like her cousin, Mary appreciated her wealth as a gift from God and used that gift for the good of others. Unlike Barnabas, Mary remained in one place and her house became a home base for fellow believers.

When Peter was freed from prison, he knocked at the door of Mary's house, knowing he would be welcomed there. Mary provided

more than a shelter or meeting place. She provided a haven of acceptance for all.

The servant girl Rhoda, in her excitement, left Peter outside. She ran to tell the others, who did not believe her. Presumably Mary had just as much difficulty believing that God could bring Peter safely out of prison to her door. She probably identified with Rhoda's disbelief. Scripture makes no mention of Mary reading Rhoda the riot act for shutting the door in Peter's face. I admire the respect implied by that. It is possible to be in a position of authority and still have humility. I envision Mary considering Rhoda her equal in Christian fellowship in spite of their employer/employee relationship.

Occupation, economic status, education, ethnicity, neighborhood: any number of circumstances determine status in society. Being a Christian calls us to treat others with respect, regardless of where they stand in relation to us in society's pecking order. It also invites us to maintain self-respect independent of our own status or lack thereof. Mary did not have a starring role in Scripture, but her contribution was significant.

Learning to Let Go

By living out her faith, Mary raised her son, John Mark, to know and serve God. Although parents cannot control their grown children's decisions, undoubtedly Mary's example played a significant role in John Mark's development. Like Barnabas and Paul, John Mark was called to spread the Good News to other communities.

Mary was given the equally challenging task of letting her son go. This was no small task. I wonder how Mary felt when John Mark left with Barnabas and Paul on their first missionary trip together (see Acts 12:25; 13:1–5). Knowing her son was accompanying his cousin Barnabas may have eased her feelings somewhat, but a mother's loving concern and protective instincts are strongly rooted.

It is hard to let go and allow our children to begin making their own way in the world. Each time a child takes another step toward independence, no matter how appropriate the time and circumstances, it takes faith and courage on the part of the parent to back off and let go. My daughter's first day of kindergarten was harder for me than for her and that was only the beginning.

It is even harder to let older children take responsibility for their own conduct. What if they make a wrong choice? However, attempts to keep grown children from making mistakes don't protect them in the long run. Such attempts deny the children the opportunity to develop their own judgment and skills. It robs them of the assurance that they can be competent without Mom or Dad. Learning this can be one of the biggest challenges for parents.

John Mark abandoned his first missionary trip, leaving Barnabas and Paul to carry on without him (see Acts 13:13). We aren't told why John Mark headed home; however, Scripture does say he accompanied Barnabas on a subsequent trip, albeit over Paul's objection (see Acts 15:37–40). Ultimately we hear Paul referring to John Mark as a coworker (see Colossians 4:10; Philemon 1:24). Paul even requested Timothy to send John Mark to him as a helper (see 2 Timothy 4:11). Peter also mentions John Mark with affectionate appreciation (see 1 Peter 5:13). In spite of what appears to be a failed first attempt to harvest in God's vineyard, John Mark ultimately became a valuable part of the early Christian ministry.

Still, I wonder how Mary felt when her son returned home after abandoning his first venture. I can imagine John Mark feeling weighed down by a sense of failure. Was Mary tempted to protect him from further failure? I might have been. On the other hand, I can't help but believe it was his mother's encouragement that sustained him and helped him develop his own inner resources.

As the mother of John Mark, Mary made a difference, if only by her example of service to fellow believers. Neither she nor any parent can take ultimate responsibility for their children's choices, since God has given all individuals free will. Nevertheless, it is reassuring to see that doing our best to share our faith with our children can have its influence.

Mary kept the home fires burning for her son, her servants, and her fellow believers. We can provide a welcoming haven for those God puts in our lives. Whether or not we have a house to share with others, we can make a home for them in our hearts.

Questions for Reflection and Discussion
1. Mary opened her home to other believers. Think of a time when others extended the grace of hospitality to you. What did you most appreciate about that experience?
2. Name some ways to extend hospitality that don't necessarily require a physical building.
3. The fact that Mary had at least one servant did not prevent her from living as a Christian. When a person has legitimate authority over others, how can he or she act with Christian charity toward them?
4. As a parent, Mary faced the challenge of letting go of her grown son along with the outcome of his decisions. In what ways does faith make letting go of our loved ones easier? In what ways might it make letting go harder?

CHAPTER TWENTY-SEVEN

Lydia
Successful Businesswoman

We set sail from Troas and took a straight course to Samothrace, the following day to Neapolis, and from there to Philippi, which is a leading city of the district of Macedonia and a Roman colony. We remained in this city for some days. On the sabbath day we went outside the gate by the river, where we supposed there was a place of prayer; and we sat down and spoke to the women who had gathered there. A certain woman named Lydia, a worshiper of God, was listening to us; she was from the city of Thyatira and a dealer in purple cloth. The Lord opened her heart to listen eagerly to what was said by Paul. When she and her household were baptized, she urged us, saying, "If you have judged me to be faithful to the Lord, come and stay at my home." And she prevailed upon us....

After [the authorities] had given [Paul and Silas] a severe flogging, they threw them into prison and ordered the jailer to keep them securely....

The police reported these words to the magistrates, and they were afraid when they heard that they were Roman citizens; so they came and apologized to them. And they took them out and asked them to leave the city. After leaving the prison they went to Lydia's home; and when they had seen and encouraged the brothers and sisters there, they departed. (Acts 16:11–15, 23, 38–40)

Taking Care of Business

Lydia was a businesswoman from Thyatira, a city in Asia Minor. Her business took her to Philippi. Located in Macedonia, not only was Philippi in another country, it was on another continent, hundreds of miles away from her home. Paul had been in Asia Minor, where Lydia lived. He wanted to preach there, but the Holy Spirit did not let him. Instead, in a vision, Paul saw a Macedonian begging, "Come over to Macedonia and help us" (see Acts 16:6–10).

Paul and Lydia both had been in Asia Minor. Why not connect there? Maybe Lydia's business obligations made it crucial for her to be in Philippi. We don't know why she ran her own business. Whether never married, widowed, or abandoned by a husband, she apparently needed to support herself. She had additional responsibilities. Her entire household depended on her for their livelihood. Willing to meet her obligations, Lydia did what she needed to do. In God's perfect timing, she did not miss the opportunity of encountering Paul.

Lydia's thirst for God was evident. She joined with other believers on the sabbath although any number of factors might have dissuaded her from worship. She may have been tired from travel or the demands of business. She was away from the structure of home. Apparently there was no synagogue in Philippi, which implies there were no male Jews acting as spiritual leaders. Nevertheless, devout women gathered to observe the Sabbath and Lydia joined them.

What about Paul? As mentioned earlier, he had wanted to stay in Asia Minor preaching, but the Holy Spirit interfered with his plan. Instead, Paul was prompted to go to Macedonia. He ended up in Philippi and spent several days there, presumably with little to show for it. On the Sabbath he went to the riverside, where Jews would gather for prayer, but found no men, only a modest gathering of women. Maybe the absence of Jewish men in Philippi made Paul more willing to sharing the Good News with women.

Perhaps Lydia needed to be out of her home element in order to be more open to Paul's message. Time away from friends, family, and familiar comforts can increase open-mindedness. The results of Lydia's business in Philippi might have contributed to her receptivity. If business went poorly, fear and discouragement may have prompted her to seek hope and solace. If business went well, gratitude may have drawn her closer to God. In any event, she listened intently to what Paul had to say and responded immediately.

Lydia was a woman of action. The same acumen and decisiveness that enabled her to succeed in business moved her to act on the truth when she heard it. She did not remain on the fence or delay in being baptized. The public nature of her actions demonstrated wholehearted willingness to be identified as a follower of Christ. There was to be no turning back.

After she and her household had been baptized, Lydia followed through. She persuaded Paul and his companions to stay in her home. I wonder why they needed persuading. Maybe they did not want to trouble her. Maybe they were afraid of a scandal. Lydia used salesmanship in her invitation, saying, "*If* you have judged me to be faithful to the Lord, come and stay at my home." If they were confident her heart was in the right place, they need not fear putting her out. If they were confident her faith was genuine, they need not fear any cause for scandal.

It was Lydia's joy to offer hospitality, in genuine gratitude for the blessings she and her household received. I suspect Lydia also may have opened her home in order to spend more time with her spiritual mentors. You can learn a lot about a person by being under the same roof and observing how they live out their faith. Attitudes are caught, not taught.

As a businesswoman in a culture where few women took leading roles, Lydia's courage and assertiveness enabled her to stand her

ground in the face of possible repercussions. Paul and Silas were arrested, beaten and thrown in jail in Philippi. Upon their release, they went straight to Lydia's house, trusting in her loyalty. She welcomed them, providing a place for them to meet with believers before they moved on (see Acts 16:16–40).

We don't know what Lydia did after Paul and his companions left. But the book of Revelation mentions the church in Thyatira as one of the seven churches in John's vision (see Revelation 2:18–29). It seems quite possible that, at some point, Lydia returned to Thyatira, and helped establish a church there.

Example of Success

I find Lydia's experience rich with insight for us today. Without success, Lydia could not have extended hospitality to believers. Worldly success does not prevent faithful devotion and Christian service. While passing through Jericho, Jesus sought out and accepted the hospitality of Zacchaeus, a rich tax collector. His success was not the problem; his dishonesty was.

Following his encounter with Jesus, Zacchaeus announced his intent to give half of his wealth to the poor and to make ample restitution to anyone he had cheated. At that point Jesus acknowledged that salvation had come to Zacchaeus and his household (see Luke 19:1–9). Zacchaeus's wealth enabled him to provide for Jesus.

Similarly, Lydia's thriving business would have enabled her not only to extend hospitality but also to travel wherever God needed her to go. Lydia did not take her career as the sole driving force of her life. She put God first, and used her business skills and resources to spread the good news. Successful career professionals have a place in God's plan today. Like Lydia, we can balance our efforts to achieve in the workplace with our efforts to grow closer to God and serve him.

Those of us who are not in the business world can still model Lydia's hospitality. It doesn't take money to create a welcoming atmosphere.

We can share what we have with generosity and kindness, even if all we have to offer is a smile to someone who needs it.

When obligations required Lydia to be away from home she still received the opportunity meant for her. We don't have to be afraid of missing out when our responsibilities necessitate a change in our plans. God knows all about our obligations and detours. He's got it covered. Lydia received the opportunities God gave her and made good use of them. May we do the same.

Questions for Reflection and Discussion

1. Paul and Lydia encountered each other in a continent far away from their homelands. Although it does not seem expedient, there was a reason for them meeting the way they did. When have you observed the wisdom of God's plan surpass what logic might indicate? How can this awareness bolster your faith?

2. In spite of factors that might have dissuaded Lydia from worshiping in Philippi, she persevered. What factors can deter or interfere with your ability to pray and worship? How do you deal with them?

3. Lydia met her obligations and did not miss out on the opportunity for spiritual growth that occurred when she met Paul. When have you experienced fear of missing out on an opportunity? What happened? How can Lydia's experience encourage you?

4. Lydia used the personal and material resources available to her as a businesswoman to benefit the Christian community. Which of your resources can you use to benefit the body of Christ?

Note: The author is indebted to Charles Spurgeon for some of the insights in this chapter.

CHAPTER TWENTY-EIGHT

Priscilla
Partner in Blessings and Risks

After this Paul left Athens and went to Corinth. There he found a Jew named Aquila, a native of Pontus, who had recently come from Italy with his wife Priscilla, because Claudius had ordered all Jews to leave Rome. Paul went to see them, and, because he was of the same trade, he stayed with them, and they worked together—by trade they were tentmakers....

After staying there for a considerable time, Paul said farewell to the believers and sailed for Syria, accompanied by Priscilla and Aquila. At Cenchreae he had his hair cut, for he was under a vow. When they reached Ephesus, he left them there, but first he himself went into the synagogue and had a discussion with the Jews. When they asked him to stay longer, he declined; but on taking leave of them, he said, "I will return to you, if God wills." Then he set sail from Ephesus....

Now there came to Ephesus a Jew named Apollos, a native of Alexandria. He was an eloquent man, well versed in the scriptures. He had been instructed in the Way of the Lord; and he spoke with burning enthusiasm and taught accurately the things concerning Jesus, though he knew only the baptism of John. He began to speak boldly in the synagogue; but when Priscilla and Aquila heard him, they took him aside and explained the Way of God to him more accurately. And when he wished to cross over to Achaia, the believers encouraged him and wrote to the disciples to welcome him.

> On his arrival he greatly helped those who through grace had become believers, for he powerfully refuted the Jews in public, showing by the scriptures that the Messiah is Jesus. (Acts 18:1–3, 18–21, 24–28)

A Real Team Player

Priscilla is mentioned several times in Scripture—always with her husband, Aquila. Like Paul, they were Jewish tentmakers and successful. They lived in Rome and then, after being expelled, relocated to Corinth. Both cities were thriving business and cultural centers, subject to the moral excesses that are so often bred in prosperity. In this environment, Priscilla and Aquila maintained their marriage as a true partnership.

Priscilla worked and traveled with her husband. Together they opened their home to believers, equally sharing the risks involved. Despite the demands of their business and the luxury their success brought with it, this husband-and-wife team had deep faith. They risked reputation, security, and life itself in order to extend hospitality and stand with fellow believers. Despite their Jewish background, they reached out to Gentile believers as well. Their financial security demonstrated powerfully that Christianity was not just for the poor, the sick, or those with nothing to lose.

Priscilla and Aquila had been uprooted from their comfortable lifestyle, first in Rome, and then in Corinth. They pulled up stakes and went to Ephesus with Paul. They remained in Ephesus when Paul moved on. What made them settle in Ephesus? Was it poor health? Old age? I wonder if they were just tired of moving. Maybe Paul's pace was too hectic or his style too bold for them. Whether due to inner motivation or external circumstances, they were not called to remain continually on the move. After several relocations, they settled and served in the community of believers in Ephesus.

In Paul's absence, when Apollos, another enthusiastic and powerful speaker of "the Way" came, Priscilla and Aquila were not swayed by his eloquence, but had the insight and courage to correct and instruct him more accurately. I love their humility in going about it. They did not share Paul's gift for oratorical flamboyance. They did not challenge Apollos publicly in the synagogue. Instead, they welcomed him into their home. In that privacy, they supplied him with the information he lacked without judgment or criticism. Apollos's heart, like theirs, was in the right place. He was able to make use of their constructive criticism and then followed his call to move on and preach.

Although only mentioned in connection with her husband, Priscilla's ministry was not lessened by his. Her risks and her service were just as real and personal as if she had acted as an individual. Her call was to serve as part of a married team. Many people serve in the single state. Some, even though married, are unable, for various reasons, to minister in close conjunction with their spouses. But Priscilla and Aquila demonstrate the blessing that can be brought forth when marriage is a vocation.

Scripture doesn't mention whether or not Priscilla and Aquila had children. If they were childless, I wonder how Priscilla felt about it. How did she feel about relocating, not once, but twice? In any event, Priscilla, a true helpmate for her husband, apparently nurtured her marriage and was nurtured by it. She did not seem driven to act more independently. Nor was she so absorbed in her love for her husband that there was little room left for outsiders. Their joint ministry helped believers as well as their marriage.

Loving God, Ourselves, and Others
Many of us face the challenges Priscilla did. Whether married or not, we may need to relocate, perhaps because of employment, economic, or other circumstances beyond our control. We might be reluctant

to accept—might even resent—being forced to give up a familiar or comfortable lifestyle. Being expelled from a major city like Rome may have seemed like a step down for Priscilla, but according to God's plan, it was just the beginning of more important things.

Maybe we mourn a childless or loveless marriage or state in life. We might struggle with surrendering our will at times for the sake of our spouses or other loved ones. It is OK to feel whatever we do feel about our circumstances. After all, God created us to have feelings. We can bring our feelings, whatever they may be, safely to God and allow him to lead us through them.

God can teach our hearts to balance loving others with loving—not losing—ourselves in a relationship. True partnership implies two full participants. Constantly putting ourselves first is wrong, of course, but it seems to me that constantly yielding to our partner can be just as detrimental as never yielding.

Jesus quoted Leviticus 19:18 when he said that the second most important commandment was to "love your neighbor as yourself" (Matthew 22:39). He did not say to love your neighbor *instead of* yourself. Sacrificially loving another is not the same as automatically putting them in first place. Jesus also affirmed Deuteronomy 6:5 when he said that the most important commandment was to " 'love the Lord your God with all your heart, and with all your soul, and with all your mind' " (Matthew 22:37–38). God belongs in first place. He is the one who can teach us when and how to balance meeting our own needs with caring for those we love.

Learning this balance is a process. Feelings of all types are bound to arise during this process. This is part of the human condition. While we can only speculate on what Priscilla might have felt, we know what she chose to do. That can encourage us to take heart, no matter what we feel about circumstances beyond our control. We are not responsible for our feelings, but for our choices. Realizing that there's

a larger purpose in whatever circumstances we experience can help us accept our feelings and move forward.

Questions for Reflection and Discussion
1. With her husband, Priscilla had to pull up stakes and leave behind all that was familiar to her when she moved from Rome and again when she moved from Corinth. In your faith journey, what have you had to leave behind? What helped you cope with the change? What did you gain?
2. When Priscilla and Aquila noticed Apollos's lack of information, they did not ignore it nor did they confront him in public. Instead, they invited him into their home. Why is a respectful and loving approach an effective way of correcting someone else? What prevents this type of approach? What encourages it?
3. Priscilla and Aquila were partners in earning their livelihood and in sharing the good news. What qualities are needed in order to work in harmony with others? Which of these qualities comes easily to you? Which would you like to develop? What would help you grow in these areas?
4. Priscilla's relationship with her husband did not seem to compete with her ability to reach out to others. Name some ways your intimate relationships can enhance, rather than compete with, loving and serving others.

Barbara Jean Hosbach is a writer whose articles have appeared in publications such as *St. Anthony Messenger, Liguorian, My Daily Visitor,* and on the web at Today's Catholic Woman. She has worked with RCIA programs since 1997, first as a sponsor, then as a catechist and retreat facilitator, and holds a B.A. in psychology from Kean University.